# Unbecoming

RIOT OF ROSES
PUBLISHING HOUSE
SEJATNGA
UNCEDED TONGVA TERRITORY
SOUTH WHITTIER, CALIFORNIA

**Published by Riot of Roses Publishing House**
**Unbecoming: Poems and Visual Art**



*ISBN (paperback): 978-1-961717-43-5*
*ISBN (ebook): 978-1-961717-44-2*

**First Edition, 2026**



To request permissions, you may contact the Publisher at *riotofrosesllc@gmail.com*
For bookings or interviews, contact:
*pam.concepcion5@gmail.com*

**Printed in the United States of America**

Edited by *Anastasia Helena Fenald* and *Brenda Vaca*
Cover Design and *Art by Justine Gabriela "Ja" S. Amores*
Layout Design by *waseem@arrowupz.com*

# advanced praise

Pam's signature prosaic style demands a slow down, a close look, a think-deeply-and-pause before doing the next thing. She draws us into an all-night conversation about what we give up to keep up, to move up. We find out it's memories, culture and love–our essence– that's being sucked out over time  measured in salary hours. We find out it's a poor trade.
– **T. Thomas,** Author, *Jeweled Scarabs*

Through Pam's echoing inner voice, culture, and metaphors, she draws us into this wonderful coming of age poetic story. We are no longer merely readers. We find ourselves becoming inside observers walking along the path of her stories. We can hear the songs, taste the food, and see the landscape through each poetic verse. She paints a vividly colorful tapestry of how our day-to-day lives are shaped and intertwined in a tango with the world around us. As a poet, I find myself hanging on to every word. Each stanza holds insight joy, humor and at times, sadness. Pam is a great storyteller and a wonderful human being who writes with love, passion and intention.
– **Marilyn "Quinoaa" Wilson Hamasu,** Poet/Author, *Earth Immigrant*

Unbecoming traces the journey of self-discovery through the lens of femininity. Concepcion explores both the tender and the turbulent moments of becoming a woman in a world that struggles to bear the weight of authentic feminism. Through revelation and self-awareness, Unbecoming gives texture and dimension to what it means to find, and free oneself.
– **Andrés Sánchez,** Author, *This Body*

*Unbecoming* clears out the naive self to make way for the honest and eager poet (un)learning to love, split between the curling streets of Manila and Los Angeles. In Pam's head-garden, we find the meaning of home. A soul demanding love beyond capitalist schedules from stability-obsessed cities and irrational lovers. She confesses, retracts, aches, and confesses again– trying to love full-time. Where do you see yourself in five years? In love, hopefully.
– **Iván Salinas,** poet and Co-Editor of *Drifter Zine*

My favorite art experiences have always been those that ferry me to a world I could never have gotten to on my own, and so it is with *Unbecoming*. To experience Pam Concepcion's writing as words artfully arranged on a page is only part of its pleasuring. Her poetry calls for

you to wrap your arms around it and listen to its whispers. Invites you to inhale it like aromas from your mama's kitchen. Seduces you like a lover who says out loud what you have never admitted to yourself. Pam's poetry does not seem written, it seems she has dreamed it into existence. To experience this book is to dream along.
– **Mike Bonifer,** Author, *White Men My Age*

*Unbecoming*, an inspired unveiling that reads like a trip towards self-discovery. the pieces feel like they're finding some beauty inside of what at first, feels unmet or ugly. A sense of something *transformative* with the author and the reader seems simultaneous, while taking in this thorough write-through of self-doubt to self-realization.
– **Maestro Gamin,** Poet

Pam built gardens in verse that are explored overnight as a means of reflection on the consequences of capitalism. The act of unbecoming creates talks on reaching for stars, rationality, comparative and contradictory observations of natural disasters in a woman's lifetime, imperfection, etc. To unbecome is also to be human.
– **Jesse Tovar,** Writer, Founding editor of *Mobile Data Mag*, and *Systemic Dreaming*

In Pam Concepcion's *Unbecoming*, one feels the intensity of her experiences as a woman in a world that wants her to be everything but who she truly is, that tries to dictate how she should live. Concepcion exquisitely bridges the personal and the political through poems such as *"love & late-stage capitalism"*, revealing the heartbreaking cost of societal pressures on desire, identity, and selfhood."
– **Brian Dunlap,** Founder and Editor-in-Chief of Los Angeles Literature, Author, *Concrete Paradise*

*to the little kids*
*we've left behind*
*in the closets of our mind,*
*these words are yours to find*
*your way back home*

*

*para kay Lola Yolly*

# contents

## attempts at living & loving

# introduction

*When I let go of what I am, I become what I might be.*
*- Lao Tzu*

We are in constant states of becoming and unbecoming. Like teenagers following the trends of time, we are continuously reinventing ourselves to find our identity, and ultimately, our place in the world. As we go through these cycles of change, our relationships with our immediate environment evolve accordingly.

This collection of poems and images is a coming-of-age story, exploring the complexities of creating the self both externally and internally. We grow up absorbing our own milieux, influencing our concepts of self: from beauty, sexuality, love, career, beliefs, and philosophies. While we conceptually build worlds in our minds, we also learn to iteratively navigate these worlds in another cycle of conforming and resisting.

Having heard "how unbecoming of a woman!" or "kababae mong tao pero..." in many variations– spoken and unspoken, I feel I have unbecome countless of times, after having once become myself. Now I am here, constantly figuring out: *How does one become a woman? What constitutes being a woman? How does a woman see the world?*

In the world I happened to build, it seems there is a tension between living and loving; needing to forego one for the other. As a kid, I was taught to act from a place of love and empathy, so I did. At the same time, I was taught to conceal emotions, to be tough, to be a man, so we can live to see the "Real World," so I also did. These conflicting notions left me wondering whether it's possible to create a world where we can live and love without sacrificing the other.

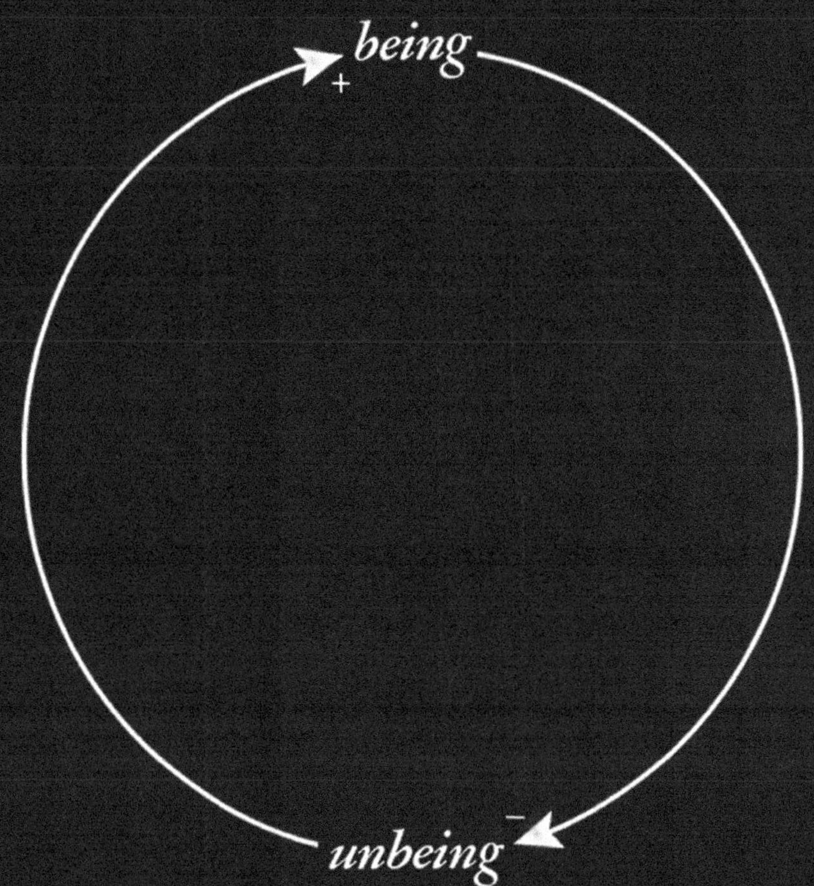
being
+
–
unbeing

# la niña

I am not woman.
I am not human.
I am a typhoon of feelings.
Forecasted and fear
mongered on the news.
Named and numbered
before Christmas.
I clear out grocery shelves
and bring out rosary spells.

From remnants of equatorial heat,
I form clouds in the tropical southeast.
Revolting rainfall revealing leaks you never knew
existed in the ceilings of your concrete sealed psyche.
I flood the floors of your architectural routines,
until the water level rises to the heart
of your day so you either wait
for the riverside carabao statues to emerge
or wade through towering waters.

Find the calm within me,
and meet me
eye to eye.

*opposite: dalagita - family archives*

# i finally feel pretty!

I was in the sixth grade
when I first said it out loud.
Something I'd never felt
for twelve years.

I had just gotten my hair          straightened
for the first time
I rushed home,
hid in my room,
& took a photo of myself          *smiling*
so this cute boy could see
how I could be pretty,
like those hot girls in magazines and TV.

It was always a mystery
how my family had hair
so silky, smooth, & straight
while mine turned
frizzy, dry, & *wild,*
despite being born with a crown
so silky, smooth, & straight
like everyone else's.

My mother told me it was *damaged;*
it had to be "tamed."
Some said it was poofy like a poodle's.
Others said instant noodles,
one said *pubes.*

Day and night, I brushed my hair
head upside down
to let the blood rush–
A friend said     it helps?

I tried it all:
boar brush, round brush, paddle brush, wide-tooth comb,
fine-tooth comb, Tangle Teezer, Denman.

I did leave-in treatments
while watching a chief justice's impeachment.
So far, I've put to trial:

*opposite: undefined roots - family archives*

baby oil, olive oil, coconut oil, mayonnaise, egg whites
as instructed by monthly magazines
in hopes of "taming the wild"
yet not one doing me justice.

I went through cycles of
pretty & ugly &
pretty & ugly &
pretty & ugly until

I grew tired

of avoiding my reflection
while sitting in the salon
for hours & hours
every four months.
My genes, refusing to submit
to the chemical altering
burning my scalp, leaving a mark
of guilt
for spending
my mother's money

only to rush home,
hide in my room,
& cry,
never feeling pretty enough
like I first did in the sixth grade.



*opposite: curl defining – self-portrait by pam*

# deconsecration

Can I separate body from *Soul*
like church and state? Is there a way
to deconsecrate– Don't take this,
all of you, don't eat of it.

This is Not My body
It will be given up
by Me. My skin constricts Me.
My bones constrain Me.

I'm a captive to My own shape,
as if I am only molded
for the tangible & the visible– *No.*
I crave power beyond touch.

Every gaze at this temple
of a body is filled with *so much awe,*
yet no one has dared to offer prayer.
Can the Soul be released

from flesh but remain human?

# a reading on a child's ritual of peeing

On Sunday mornings,
my mother taught me
how to pee in public restrooms.

I tug-tug-tug at her blouse, ripping
her mind away from prayer.
She bows her head to hear
my whispered pleas:
*"mommy...* *wiwi."*

She lets out a sigh.
Giant bag in one hand,
my hand in the other,
as we shuffle out of the pews.

Cramped in a cubicle
made only to be stood in,
my mother preaches
a gospel I would be needing
for my growing years.

I wasn't old enough
to tippy toe over toilets
the way she does
so, she carries me by the waist,
hovers me over the porcelain mouth,
then instructs me:
Put your feet on either side of the seat.
Pull your panties down to your knees.
Scrunch your dress up to your chest.
Squat–
Hold on to your undies.
Give way to the incoming stream.
*Pee*

but never *ever* touch the bowl!
She stood in front,
holding me through the whole ordeal.

As she cleans me up
and puts me down,
we hear distant voices entering
and echoing in the stall:
*"Praise to You, Lord Jesus Christ."*

# swimming lessons

I'm still learning
how to tread this ocean heart carefully,
so I can consume the waves instead
of them crashing over me.
I let my hands raisin wrinkle
as the current carries my cries.
Salty streams teardrop my goggles full,
forcing closed eyes to find surface & sky.

On calmer days, I would dive
deeper than my lungs can handle.
Down aquatic residences of coral reefs colored,
in irrational rainbows I never see on land,
schools of fish, glimpses of sirens–
I'm almost pulled into their world
but bubbles escape my mouth,
reeling me back to the air, reminding me
to breathe.

I used to be jealous of my older siblings;
they took swimming lessons as kids,
learned all the strokes
to direct themselves in the water.
My dad said I didn't need them. I naturally
floated away on my own
as a baby.

Water surrounded my home–
Surrender was my only choice.
I never felt the need
to swim against the heart          until
the age of inheritance.          I gained

paternal fears: the knowledge
of drowning if I swam farther
than my mother can see
& getting caught in riptides.
So, I declared El Niño & stopped          swimming.

Pam Concepcion

I stayed by the shore with my mom,
scraping sand against calloused skin
to soften and smoothen hardened husks;
wading waist-level weakened waves to wash
wounds from broken bottles buried;
buoying in bubble barriered leisure zones;
floating in life-vest snorkel safety—
refusing to navigate
deep-sea conflicts
in uncharted trenches.

Yet water surrounds my home—
Surrender *is* my only choice & now
I'm all rusty, relying
on muscle memory, remembering
my lungs aren't a muscle & I keep forgetting to *breathe.*

I'm still learning
how to tread my ocean heart
carefully.
My dad said I'm a natural.
I guess I'll just float away
like a baby.



*opposite: swimming ladies – painting by ja amores*

# laro lang

Noong ako'y dose anyos,
walang pinagkaiba ang katawan ko
sa mga kalaro kong lalaki,
puwera lang sa'ming pag-ihi.
Lahat kami'y pantay-pantay
ng mga ulo't balikat, maliban sa ibang
matatangkad ang magulang.

Matapos ang aming klase sa hapon,
mga lulod at tuhod nami'y nag-iipon
ng sugat sa ilalim ng pantalong
puro mantsa ng lupa at dugo.

Walang sawang laro nang laro nang laro,
araw-araw nang suot ang PE uniform ko.
Mas mabilis kasi akong tumakbo
kapag hindi ako naka palda.

Hindi pa ako dalaga,
tinanong ako ng nanay ko
sa tonong ginagamit niya
tuwing may kasalanan ako:
"Bakit hindi ka na nagpapalda?
*Tomboy ka ba?"*

Naalala ko ang bespren kong babae na
maikli ang buhok
at laging naka pantalon.
May mali ba siyang ginawa?

Pero ako? Tomboy? Hala! Ang haba kaya ng hair ko!
*Hindi!* sagot ko agad,
sabay tumahimik– walang imik pauwi
at kinalimutan ang kuwento
kung paano ko nilampasan
ang bawat lalaki
sa takbuhan.

# all fun and games

At twelve years old,
my body was no different
from the boys I played with–
besides the way we peed.
We all stood the same height
and carried the same weight.

Once the school bell rings,
knees and shins gathered
scrapes and wounds beneath pants
stained with dirt and blood.

Every day we played and played and played,
I had to wear jogging pants. I learned
I run faster when I wasn't in a skirt.

Months before my womanhood,
my mother asked me,
in the voice she used
when she caught me playing
with fire:
*"Bakit hindi ka na nagpapalda?"*
*Tomboy ka ba?!"*

I remembered my best friend. She
always wore pants
and got short haircuts.
Did she do something bad?

But me? A tomboy? I couldn't be! My hair went past my ears!
*No!* I said defensively
and kept quiet the whole ride home;
never telling her the story
of how I ran
faster
than every single boy.

# relaxing

I’ve been sitting down
for the past four hours
on the same chair
I sat on, a few months ago.
My head facing down,
staring at some magazine article
(about some celebrity
I don’t care even about)
just so I don’t have to stare
at my reflection across my chair.

I’ve probably pored
through a dozen magazines
showing the same women with hair
flowing down perfectly
with a wedding veil.
I’ve already gotten used
to the smell, but
my eyes are still
watering
because of some
chemical gel
sitting on my hair.

I can feel my scalp
b u r n i n g
which means
the gel or
whatever it is
on my head
is doing its job.
I’ll just have to
w a i t
a few more hours
so I can finally
look up, and
let my hair down.



*opposite: cover girls – collage by pam*

no boys allowed!
Watch how this tween queen grew up in the limelight!
Rachel Vs Mischa
HOT NEW FASHION!
Get Rid Of The Clutter!
Say Bye to Bad Trip Blind Dates!
HEATHER IN SHOCK: Richie Dates Denise
SPECIAL DOUBLE ISSUE
YES!
People
100 MOST BEAUTIFUL STARS
www.showbiznest.com
64 Pages
a princess!

Pam Concepcion

# field of dreams

I walk towards a box
of white chalk, lined
on freshly watered soil.

The soles of my feet
feel the heat
from beneath,
as I slide my cleats
from left to right
until common ground
is found between the two.

Through squinted eyes
and rusted grills,
I look past the ground
beyond my box
and lock my gaze
on the mound across.

As throws wound up,
pings and dings and thuds
echoed in the box.
Creating a beat
leading to a chorus         from a distance.
I hear cheers and jeers
yet my mind remains
                                        distant
from the refrain
when my fears
                              are at such a close distance.

I shifted my stance
to follow the pace
of the pacing rhythm,
hoping to get on base—
bracing for the throw
that throws off my rhythm.

Within two-hundred-fifty feet
from where my feet stand,
are the stands where
game winning hits often land
on someone's bare hands.

As I fix my stance in the box, I pray
today is the day
I finally reach the stands.

# menarche

Tumagos
sa isipan ko
ang araw ng aking pagdadalaga.

Maaga akong nakauwi galing eskuwela.
Huling araw na ng klase
bago ang aming Christmas party!

Matagal ko nang pinagplanuhan
ang isusuot kong damit:
Bagong blusang kulay tsokolate,
at may puting puntas,
na butas-butas ng hugis sampaguita.
Mala Maria Clarang Amerikana ang dating!
Tinerno ko 'to sa pantalong itim
na 'siya ri'y may puntas at disenyong bulaklak sa laylayan.

Linatag ko ang damit sa higaan
nang maisukat–
tila dress rehearsal
ng isang tanghalan!
Tiyak akong gandang-ganda
mga kaklase ko sa'kin bukas!

Paghubad ko ng uniporme ko,
nakita ko ang mantsa ng dugo
sa likod ng palda ko.

Ah.
*Dalaga na ako.*

# menarche

The day I *finally* became a woman
is perpetually stained
on my mind.

I got home from school early.
It was the last day of classes
before our Christmas party!

It took me *months* to plan
how I would look that day:
A brand-new blouse in a deep, chocolate-brown shade
with white, lacey, Cath Kidston-esque patterned frills,
a scooping bib around my chest
and black dress-code-friendly leggings
with floral lace trimmings at the ankle.

I laid them out on my bed
to fit the clothes
like a wedding dress
on the eve of I do's.
Tomorrow, I'm sure
my classmates will call me pretty.

As I stripped
my uniform at home,
I saw the stain
on the back of my skirt.

Oh.
*Dalaga na ako.*

## periodic expenses

| | | |
|---|---|---|
| Tricycle | ₱ | 25.00 |
| Beep card load | ₱ | 100.00 |
| 2 packs Kotex napkin with wings | ₱ | 115.00 |
| 1 pack overnight napkin with wings | ₱ | 63.50 |
| 2 packs Carefree liner | ₱ | 127.50 |
| 1 bottle feminine wash | ₱ | 57.00 |
| 1 loaf wheat bread | ₱ | 64.50 |
| 2 kg brown rice | ₱ | 135.40 |
| 1 pack white fish | ₱ | 176.00 |
| 1 can Tuna | ₱ | 54.25 |
| 1 bag Romaine Lettuce | ₱ | 42.00 |
| 2 pcs Eggplant | ₱ | 41.40 |
| 5 pcs Potatoes | ₱ | 68.40 |
| 3 pcs Carrots | ₱ | 42.75 |
| 2 pcs Fuji Apple | ₱ | 118.80 |
| 2 pcs Lemon | ₱ | 71.20 |
| 2 pcs Navel Orange | ₱ | 154.76 |
| Tricycle | ₱ | 30.00 |
| | | |
| Tricycle | ₱ | 35.00 |
| 1 bottle facial toner | ₱ | 175.00 |
| 1 pack cotton balls | ₱ | 12.10 |
| 1 pack face mask peel off | ₱ | 109.00 |
| 1 Potato Corner Jumbo fries BBQ | ₱ | 80.00 |
| 2 packs Lucky Me Pancit Canton Chilimansi | ₱ | 24.30 |
| 2 bags Potato Chips | ₱ | 46.25 |
| 1 box 3 pcs RELX Menthol Xtra 5% | ₱ | 750.00 |
| Tricycle | ₱ | 40.00 |
| | | |
| 2 C3 + 2 extra rice | ₱ | 336.00 |
| 2 large Milk Tea | ₱ | 240.00 |
| * | | |
| 1 pack disposable underwear | ₱ | 70.00 |
| 1 pair shorts | ₱ | 150.00 |
| 1 Napkin sa vendo | ₱ | 5.00 |
| Tricycle | ₱ | 50.00 |
| | | |
| TOTAL** | ₱ | 3,610.11 |

* shet
** non-food impulse purchases not included



*opposite: enlightened – collage by pam*

# kaibigan lang

Natuwa ang magulang ko
noong nalaman nilang
may gusto ako
sa isang lalaki.

Pinapayagan nila akong lumabas
kasama ng mga kalaro kong
lalaki— at baka sakaling
maging ka-date ko sa prom.

Wala akong nakatuluyan
sa mga lalaking
aking nakagustuhan.
Nang mas nakilala ko sila,
mas ginusto ko sila,
bilang kaibigan—
e, halos pareho naman
din mga gusto namin.

Sa dalas ko silang makasama,
Itinuturing nila ako bilang kanilang *pare.*
Kinatuwaan ko 'to:
*Ako?* Ang bukod-tanging *rosas sa hardin* ng tinik?!

Ngayo'y napagtanto ko:
Kaya ba hindi sila nagkagusto sa akin?

Bigla kong narinig ang mga boses
ng buong kamag-anakan ko:
*"Tomboy ka ba?"*

Pero, lagi ko namang suot
yung unipormeng palda sa eskuwelahan, ah?
Pinaputol ko pa nga lahat ng pantalon ko
para naka pekpek shorts ako
tuwing naglalaro.

Hindi pa ba ako mukhang babae?
Tumingin ako sa salamin:
"Ah, yung buhok ko kasi
buhaghag na nga,
masyadong pang maiksi.

Pati pala yung braso ko–
sabi ng tatay ko,
nasobrahan na raw sa pagpupukol.
Masyadong nang malaki,
nagmumukha na akong lalaki.

Panalo nga kami sa laro, ngunit
talo naman
sa kagandahan.

Hindi pa ata ako tapos magdalaga.

# just friends

My parents were overjoyed
when they found out *I like*
*liked* a boy.

They let me go out
with those boys I grew up with
in hopes that any one of them
would become my prom date.

I didn't end up dating
any of those boys I liked.
The more I got to know them,
I started liking them more
as friends.
We almost always liked
the same things anyway.

I spent so much time with them,
they even called me their *pare.*
and I *loved* it–
being "one of the boys"
I was *cool.*

In retrospect, I thought:
is that why they didn't like me back?

Then a chorus of familiar voices surface
from the depths of my mind:
"Tomboy ka ba?!"

But, I always wore our school-sanctioned skirts!
I cut all my pants into short-shorts
when I play sports.

Am I not woman enough yet?
I looked in the mirror:
"Oh, it must be my hair
It's too frizzy and short."

My dad also told me
my two-toned tan-lined arms
had gotten too toned
from throwing so many wins.
Everyone said I looked like him but I don't want to
look too much like a boy.

Maybe I'm not yet done
becoming a woman.

winner
4-masipag
aug 4 '09
part I.
1. True
2. False - barangay tanod
3. True
4. False - pueblo
5. True
6. True
8. True False district
10. False Pamahalaan
WOAH

# learning environment

In *my classroom,* I sit by the door
for a perfect view of hallways hedged
by thorny fuchsia bougainvillea.
Sunrays on the open field,
green grass, stretching out to a shade
of brown roots creeping; cracking pavement
in between two lines of Kalachuchi trees.
Shadows of branches dropping
white and fuchsia flowers. Past those trees, you'll only see
more trees: Acacia, Molave, Eucalyptus, Bamboo, Talisay.

*The Mini Forest*– an ecosystem that cools the warm
air enough to replace
air-conditioning systems.
Our friends from slightly colder places
jokingly made us jealous
with their jacketed classroom fashion.

If only they opened
their windows and doors
they would feel the breeze.
The leaves calmed the climate
so we could wear hoodies to hide
the fact that we weren't wearing
our IDs, a bra, or anything underneath.

In my first year of high school,
I passed the Kalachuchi walk every day
to see my senior crush
sitting on stone benches
beside her girlfriend. Petals waltzed
gracefully with gravity, landing
silently on her skirt. She tucked
the white flower behind her lover's ear.

Across them were my weird friends,
picking up dirtied leaves and flowers,
pulling the petals backwards,
pinning them down to its own stem,
creating a clover quantum field.

*opposite: passing notes - mixed media by pam*

*Sushi!* They cry as they serve eight
on a long kalachuchi leaf plate.

The trees set the scene
for horror stories and love stories alike,
inspiring freshmen to practice classic lines:
*Romeo, Romeo. Wherefore art thou Romeo?*
and juniors to confess:
*Lagi akong nagbabakasakaling babalik ka,*
*kung kaya't parati akong naghihintay*
*sa hardin na ating pinagtatagpuan.*

Two sets of star-crossed lovers,
the male role: the butch-type classmate–
always ready to act                    like their true self;
the female role: the former's crush.
A plot cast by the class
for our very own *love team.*

Our teacher told us
the trees were planted
by missionary sisters
some fifty to seventy years ago:
a time where all love and life
died a thousand deaths.
In retrospect, this made me wonder:
*How does one think of planting trees*
*amidst civil unrest?*

Months before our graduation,
one of those sisters visited us.
She said *Agape is the highest form of love.*
I wonder if she felt it in the Kalachuchi Walk.

It's beyond puppy love,
beyond unrequited love,
beyond unconditional love.
It's the kind of love that cuts
through fields                                        of space and time
like planting trees and waiting fifty-years.

The seeds she once held in her palm
have grown roots          breaking through pavement,
and branches towering thirty feet over her; nurtured
for students
                                        who are yet to be born.

*opposite: kalachuchi walk - family archives*

# beauty lessons from adults

What are you teaching your children
when you praise them for losing
weight while working through waking
hours without regard for their well-being
but wealth-making for the well-off?

What are you teaching your children
when you bring to attention
naturally occurring body hair,
making each strand visible
in passing reflections?

What are you teaching your children
when you visually measure the beauty
of their arms and waist
relative to digitally altered,
publicist-approved images,
instead of how they feel
embracing you— hiding tears
after facing fears
of failing and falling
in love with the wrong idea?

What are you teaching your children
when the first thing that comes
out of your mouth—
before *hello*
or *kamusta ka na?*[1]
is always something you see     wrong
on their body?

---

[1] how have you been?

# babaeng babae

Unti-
unti kong
binuo ang
aking pagdadalaga.

Sa loob ng tatlong taon,
mga palda't bestida ko'y nag-iipon
sa damitang punong-puno
ng damit panlaro— noon.

Sinigurado kong
kapit na kapit
ang aking damit,
sinaulo lahat ng sukat:
UK US EU JP
para makita ang
korte ng dibdib,
at ang kurbang
nagpapahalatang
maliit ang baywang.

Kahit maini't malagkit,
inilulugay ko ang buhok kong
abot dibdib kapag bagong rebond,
nang maitago ang brasong
masyadong malaki

para sa isang babae.

Sa lahat ng mga kailangan ko
para maging isang dalaga,
pinakamahalaga ang kolerete
para lumabas ang aking ganda!

Mukha ko'y isang obra ni Juan Luna.
Pinta ng linya sa mata, tila Haponesa.
Pulahan ang labi mala- Maine Mendoza.
Kulayan ang pisngi, as if laging kinikilig!
Takpan ang pinagsipagang itim sa ilalim ng mata
nang di mahalatang nagsusunog ako ng kilay.
Itago lahat ng marka ng pagkabata:
tigyawat sa noo, sa ilong, sa baba.

Ito na talaga ako! Makikita na ako
bilang isang kaakit-akit na binibini!

Bago ako lumabas ng bahay,
pinagsabihan pa nga ako ng:
*ang landi-landi mo naman!*
Di bale, hindi naman *tomboy!*

Nang makita ako ng kaibigan kong
lalaki.
Nabighani siya.
*"Aba, babae ka na."*

Sa wakas.
Dalaga na talaga ako!

# real girl

Slowly,
but surely,
I styled myself
for womanhood.

My closet, once filled with

knickers and jerseys,

had now amassed a pile of skirts and dresses.
I obsessively measured myself
in UK US EU JP
so my clothes
tightly hugged
my body to show
the shape of my chest,
and the curves to prove
I had a tiny waist.

I let my chemically straightened hair grow
past my chest. I let it down,
despite the hot and humid air,
to hide my arms

that were still too big

for a girl.

After the clothes,
the most important thing one needs
to become a woman is makeup
to bring out our *true beauty*.
I turned my face into a canvas:
Winged my eyes so they could fly.
Glittered my lids for a glammed glance.
Stained, lined, and glossed my lips.
Shaped my brows into sisters, not twins!
Painted over emotional under eyes
and hormonal acne scars.
Color, contour, conceal
to reveal:
*a princess.*

Before I left the house, I was told
*ang landi-landi mo naman!*
At least it wasn't *tomboy!*
When my best friend saw me,
he was charmed.
*"Wow. Babae ka na."*

Finally.
*Dalaga na talaga ako!*



*opposite: babae ka na! – self-portrait by pam*

FINE

# awakenings & new media sex ed

the first sex scandal in my conscious history: a Disney star/ shame coated hands searching / my touch is light / I type in whispers / childish curiosity shifts to confusion / secondhand embarrassment meets awe / a stolen glance at a body: B-cup boobs, bit of belly, black baby bush / a foreign yet familiar brown figure/ a quick peek of what I might grow into

my third-grade classmate shares a wild wide-eyed secret / she discovers *Redtube* on her brother's computer / I find myself at home / unattended latch-key inquisitions / dialing up a new forbidden fruit– so good something stirs below my stomach / thrill / two bodies / perfect skin / hairless and light / perfect shapes / chiseled, curvy, colossal / tension builds violently / man towers over woman / on her knees / the absence of passion / lust / fear / sin always tastes sweet at the first bite

local news headlines echo careless whispers circulating online / a famous *celebrity surgeon* / married / an actress from my favorite teleserye / a camera / hidden / eyes like a false god watching from above/ the scene of the affair / ecstatic entanglement of lovers recorded in lowlight secrets / sold to the markets / filed cases, court hearings, and drug probes / in finding God, he is anew and reinstated / she almost never danced again in the limelight / she's always casted a villain

a fire of high school hallway gossips set ablaze / *she was playing with herself* / the video is spreading / an alternative form of learning biology/ how did you know it's her / the face isn't even seen / why would *she* do that? / suppressing hushed judgements / who did she send it to? / who did *he* send it to? / it's just locker room group chats / harmless

*she posted it on IG!* / rumors of suspension arose / that photo isn't so bad!/ she wasn't even *fully* naked / braless, bare back, denim shorts, over the shoulder smile, beach girl style / we're 16 & learning / bodily exploration / & in dire need of a second sermon after our monthly mass / what's wrong with the photo? / *you are students of a highly respected exclusive all girls catholic school* / *we are empowering girls to be trailblazing women* / *you must be a model of what good catholic students are* / proud of our brains yet ashamed of & unacquainted with our bodies

*"History Class"* / a shared Google Drive / a visual archive by the neighboring Jesuit all-boys school / *All The Girls We've Lusted For* / an exquisite exposé on a girl's trust / so sensitive & intimate / invading pinky-promise privacies / pixel pink panties & photogenic pussies / we have no proof beyond girl talk / it's all in the cloud / some girls said / *Oo, ako rin.* [2] Can we Ctrl+Shift+Delete / All time?

[2] *Yes, me too.*

# 2020+1 tokyo olympics

We had only ever streamed games
on Facebook Live, brought to us
by a player's phone on limited mobile data.
A static wide shot of soil and grass
behind a grid of metal grills, silhouettes of players,
a *tok!*, clusters of moving pixels, static screams–
the ball is in play.
We hear exclusive bench cheers, jeers and chatters,
coaches cursing out gods, saints, and sharks–
our in-game commentary,
while we constantly comment:
*Anong inning na? Ano na score? Sinong lamang?*

Now, in this fully-funded effort
to bring back the sport,
every action captured
in high resolution. Every position covered
by at least three cameras.
It is a revolution
to my eyes: revelations of the body
at the professional level–
each fielder's frame built
to fit their function.
Seeing the rotation
of the batter's hips, waist
twisting, and arms gripping,
connecting bat to ball;
the reaction of a third baseman
as she fields a hard hit by the powdery foul line,
a suave backhanded pick-n-throw to first;
the motion of a baserunner
stealing and sliding into second base,
dusty sandy soil smoking up the screen;
the emotion of teammates cheering
each other up after an error;
and the mere reflection of bodies
that look like mine and my teammates'.

Unlike college "chicks" on local TV,
those cheerleaders in skirts,
those flexible fearless flyers

*opposite: little league – family archives*

contorting limbs on a tier, then in the air;
or those volleyball girls
serving, setting, spiking–
rallying with cold-blooded composure
in their chest-tight sleeveless jerseys,
thigh-hugging short-shorts.
Cameramen focus
on bodies so slender and petite,
tall, busty, and leggy;
faces barely sweaty;
always TV type pretty,
always a fast-selling, high-rating day
thanks to middle aged dads, caught
on camera 2, intently watching
"the game."

Our coach tells us stories
of her trips to the Little League World Series.
How All-Star American girls step up the plate,
Video and Photoready.
Hair up with red, white, and blue ribbons;
and full-face make-up:
foundation, lipstick, eyeshadow, eyeliner, mascara–
never batting an eyelash
at another team's homerun.
We see our senior *Ates*[3] bringing home
the newest Easton or Louisville bats,
Rawlings mitts and batting gloves,
Nike cleats, and jerseys designed
for *Asia Pacific.*
That league was our own Olympics–
our Field of Dreams now stored
in the equipment room
at the back of our minds
until today.

It's our turn now to step into the batter's TV box.
So, we scale internet fences and IP addresses
to tune in every zoomed-in,
slow-mo instant replay

---

[3] Ate – older sister, honorific for older female peers

of a pitch; every bead of sweat,
every speck of dirt
on sunburnt skin. It's been
two years since I last threw a fastball,
but I can feel the seams of the ball leave
my fingertips. My feet dragging
on dirt, recalling the heat
beneath my cleats, and my weight
transferring from left quad
to right toes, springing my body
into a windmill    moving forward,
                                        into a new life off the field,
                                                                        cheering
                                                                         from digital stands.

Pam Concepcion

# telling time

I'll never know when it's time
to let you go.
        I always thought it was something
        I'll never know.            When it's time,
                better things will come, though
                        I'll never know when.   *It's time*

                                                to let you go.

# rest your feet

Mommy, someday
we will fly
to Florence, Italy and see
the Birth of Venus. We will
pray in seven churches,
order more than we can eat,
and walk until our feet are sore.
So, for now,     *please*
rest your feet.

You walked more than enough
for us to march          in caps and gowns.
Let me wear your shoes.
I'll walk for us today.

I always pictured you
on your feet,
even after work
and Katipunan traffic,
never failing to cook
the kind of dish that
always kept me eating
a second dinner after long commutes
from class and softball practice.

I once thanked          God
when you called me to say
you finally bought a couch
for your first apartment over there.

Go ahead, sit down, and watch
the latest Korean drama on your list.
Rest your feet tonight.

*Nandito na ako.*[4]

---

[4] I'm here now

Pam Concepcion

I'll do all the dishes;
I'll handwash our panties.
Don't worry about it.
We wear the same shoe size.
I'll walk for us today.



*opposite: mother and child – family archives*

Pam Concepcion

# 98 watermelons worth a jackson

I always take too long counting
my change after buying something.
Cash spread out on my hand,
as I separate centavos from
pesos. While clutching the centavos in
my other palm, I sort
the Rizals, Bonifacios, & Mabinis in
their own corners. Then I
Do the same with the centavos.

Once they're sorted, only then will I add

the coins' monetary value– & if things add up,

I dump them all together in my coin holder.

I once rode a bus in a place called the City of Angels & I found myself sorting foreign bills between fingers, and coins in corners of coppers & silvers in several sizes on my palm, an hour away from the next stop. As I classed the cash, only then did I put a face value to names I've only read in math problems like: "William wants to buy 98 watermelons. Alfonso is selling it for just a Jackson. William has 3 Abes, 2 Jefferies, 6 Teddies, 1 Georgie, 3 Georges, a Lincoln, & a Hamilton. What is William's change or deficit? Should William have a Benjamin, how much change will he get?" Who the fuck's Benjamin? IDK so... I skipped it.

*pages 54-55: the only green i saw was the chalkboard – digital collage by pam*

Projected
Common Stock

# contemporary corporate conditioning 101

*"The numbers have no way of speaking*
*for themselves. We speak*
*for them. We imbue*
*them with meaning."*

- *Nate Silver, The Signal and The Noise*

In the classroom, we were told
to look at The Numbers
but we weren't taught
to look beyond the numbers.

Numbers that often amount to
a large amount of

revenue, cost,
sales, tax,
profit, loss,
margin, error,
efficiency, defects,
productivity, expenditure,
et cetera, et cetera,
et cetera...

and sometimes— just sometimes,
"environmental
or social impact."

We need to solve for a number
to prove it's getting warmer
because the heat on leather
car seats in the afternoon
does not burn
into the minds of those who
are conditioned to be
in air-conditioned rooms,
centralized and regulated
at a temperature of 23.7°C—



*pages 56-57: computation and standardization – digital collage by pam*

Isolated

from the heat outside—
that's anticipated to increase
by 2 degrees.

They sit elevated
for a dioramic view
of square rooftops
forming a city-grid
board room game,
moving miniature trucks
of consumer goods
ten blocks south
to be bought
by ant-sized pawns
walking on sidewalks
that can cook eggs
or melt shoes,
and even become a shoreline
where kids float boats
made of paper
that fall into sewers.

We need to compute for a number
that converts the 2-degree increase
in heat,
and the 0.2-meter rise
in sea levels
into a language that does not confuse
the computers coded objectives of

| maximizing | or | minimizing |
|---:|---|---:|
| revenue, | | cost, |
| sales, | | tax, |
| margin, | | loss, |
| efficiency, | | error, |
| et cetera, | | defects, |
| et cetera... | | productivity, |
| | | expenditure, |
| | | et cetera, |

and sometimes— just sometimes,
"minimizing carbon dioxide emissions."

We were told that
it will never be warm
until the benefits of
turning off the air -conditioner
and decreasing
$CO_2$ emissions
is something
we can
profit
off.



*opposite: distortion – digital manipulation by pam*

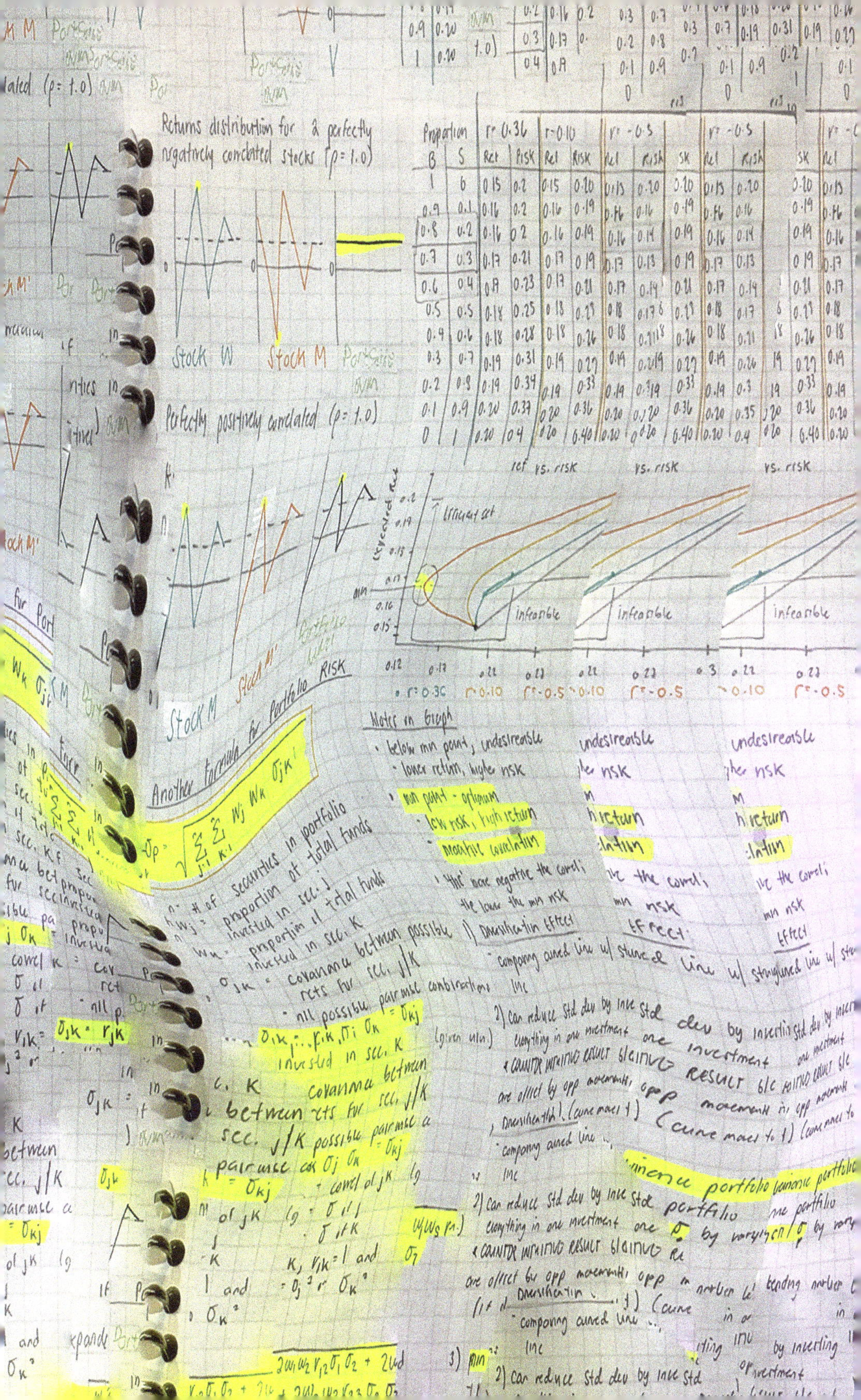
Returns distribution for a perfectly negatively correlated stocks (ρ: 1.0)
Stock W
Stock M
Portfolio WM
Perfectly positively correlated (ρ: 1.0)
Proportion
W
S
Ret
Risk
vs. risk
Efficient set
Expected rate
min
infeasible
Another formula for Portfolio RISK
n = # of securities in portfolio
wj = proportion of total funds invested in sec. j
wk = proportion of total funds invested in sec. K
σjK = covariance between possible rets for sec. j/K
Notes on Graph
below min point, undesireable
lower return, higher risk
min point - optimum
low risk, high return
negative correlation
the more negative the correl, the lower the min risk
Diversification Effect
2) can reduce std dev by investing in more than one investment
variance portfolio

# the best medicine

*Everybody is entitled to*
*a joke. Even the President is*
*entitled to a joke*

*When we say jokes*
*are half meant,*
we mean: half provoked
by its true intent,
and half in hopes
it did not offend.

The emperor is now exposed
for having no clothes
so we laugh,
*because it's true.*

We crack up jokes
with a spoonful of sugar
so we don't choke
on the bitterness
of our words, but on our laughter

diffusing the tension
of a serious and no-nonsense
set-up of a strongman. Throwing a punch-
line when least expected.

*For as long as there are many*
*beautiful women, there are plenty*
*of rape cases as well*

*The mayor should go first*

*Get hold of a picture*
*of mine and put it on*
*the altar*

*Shoot them dead*

Perhaps some laughed
because for them,

*it's true.*

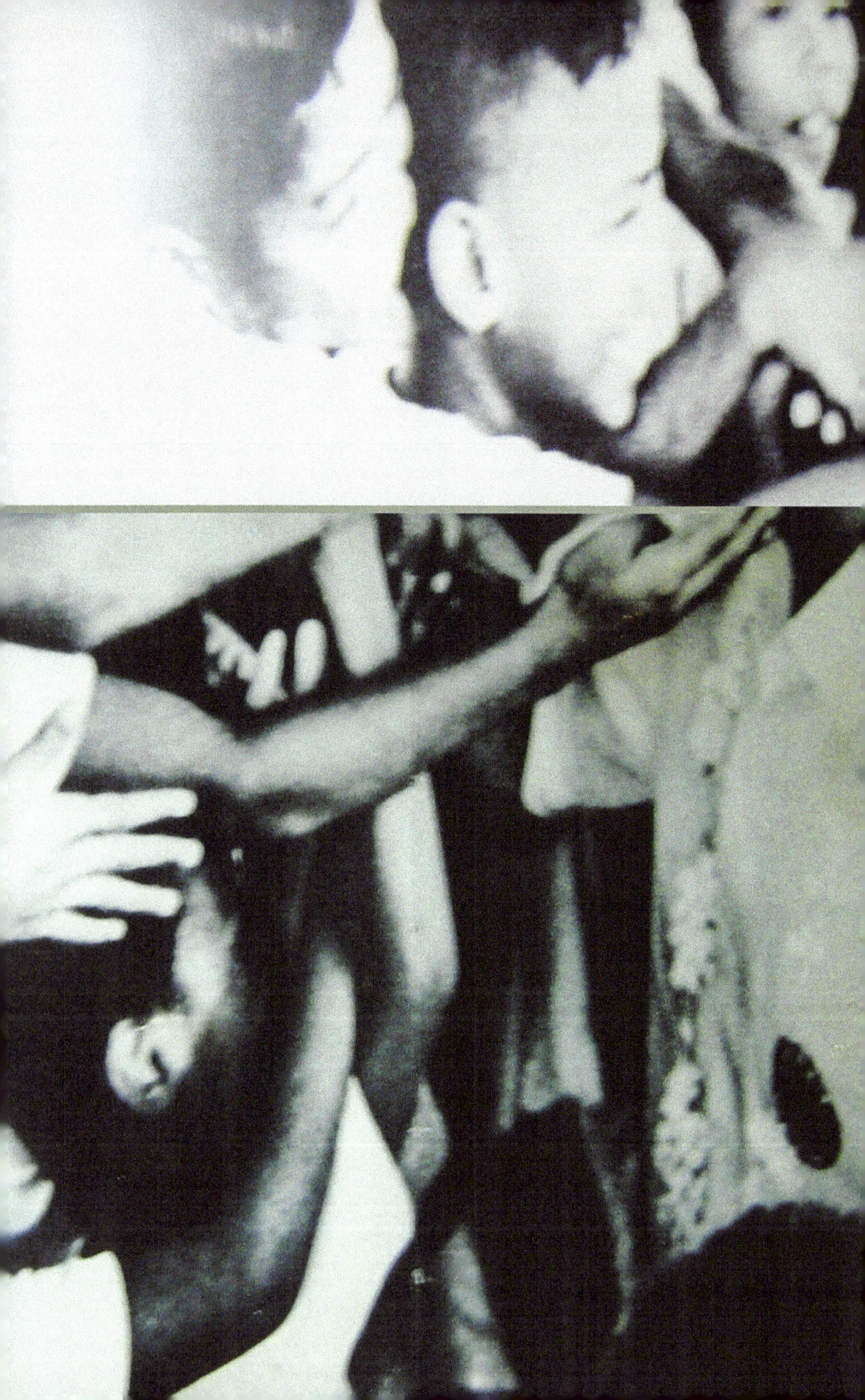

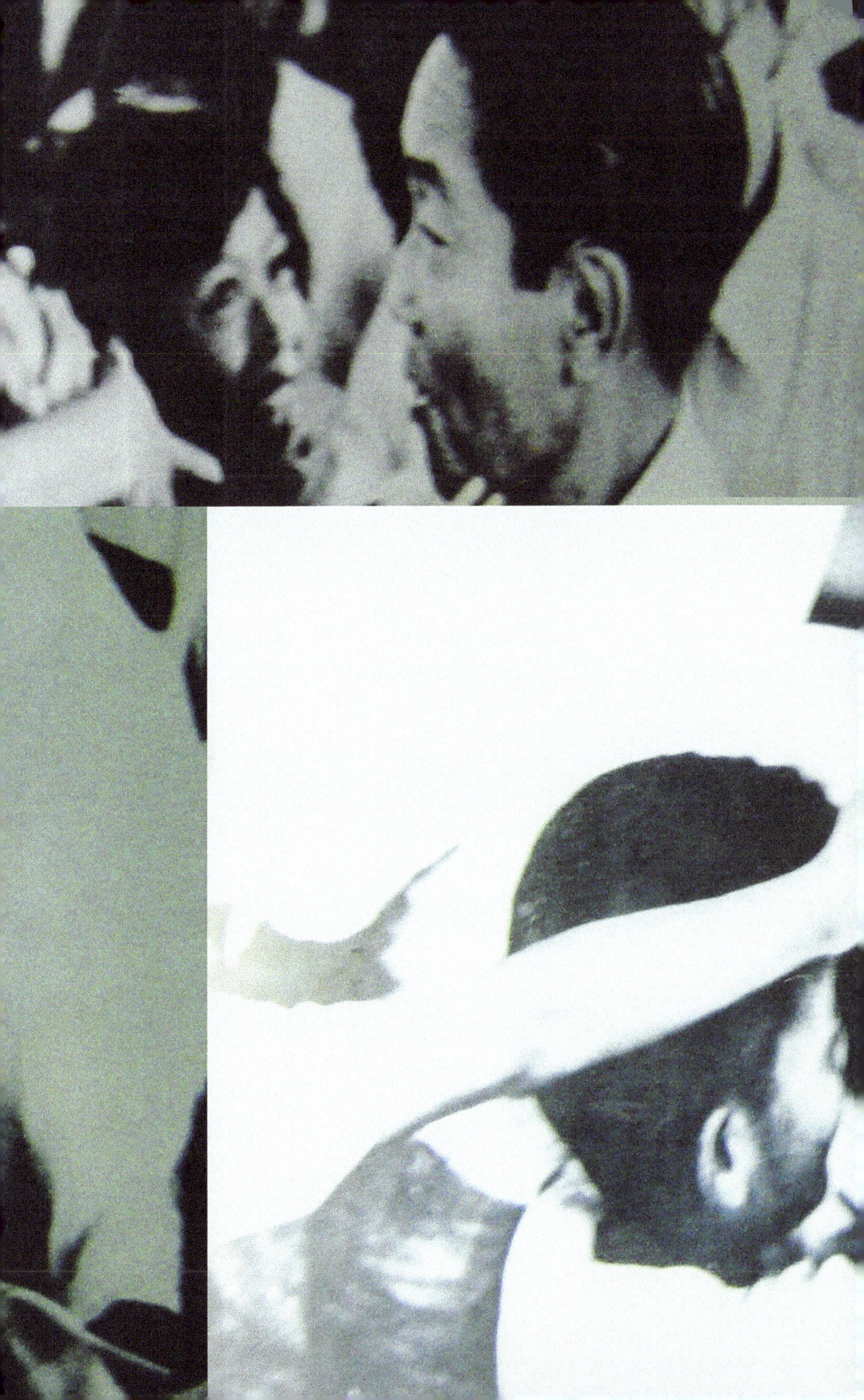

## power

*Why is it you are willing to give*
*your life for your country*
*in battle, but you refuse to give*
*her future?*

I only want

the power.

I would like to

become President.

*opposite: kayo po na nakaupo – family archives*

## all love and life

my
commonwealth demands
blood,
crime, free hands
for
strength
pride, shed
blood, burn
whatever crime,
be not mine.

my motherland calls
holocaust, I lay
down all hopes and dreams, all
love and life,
a thousand deaths and more,
and live with
pride.

*opposite: my commonwealth demands – family archives*

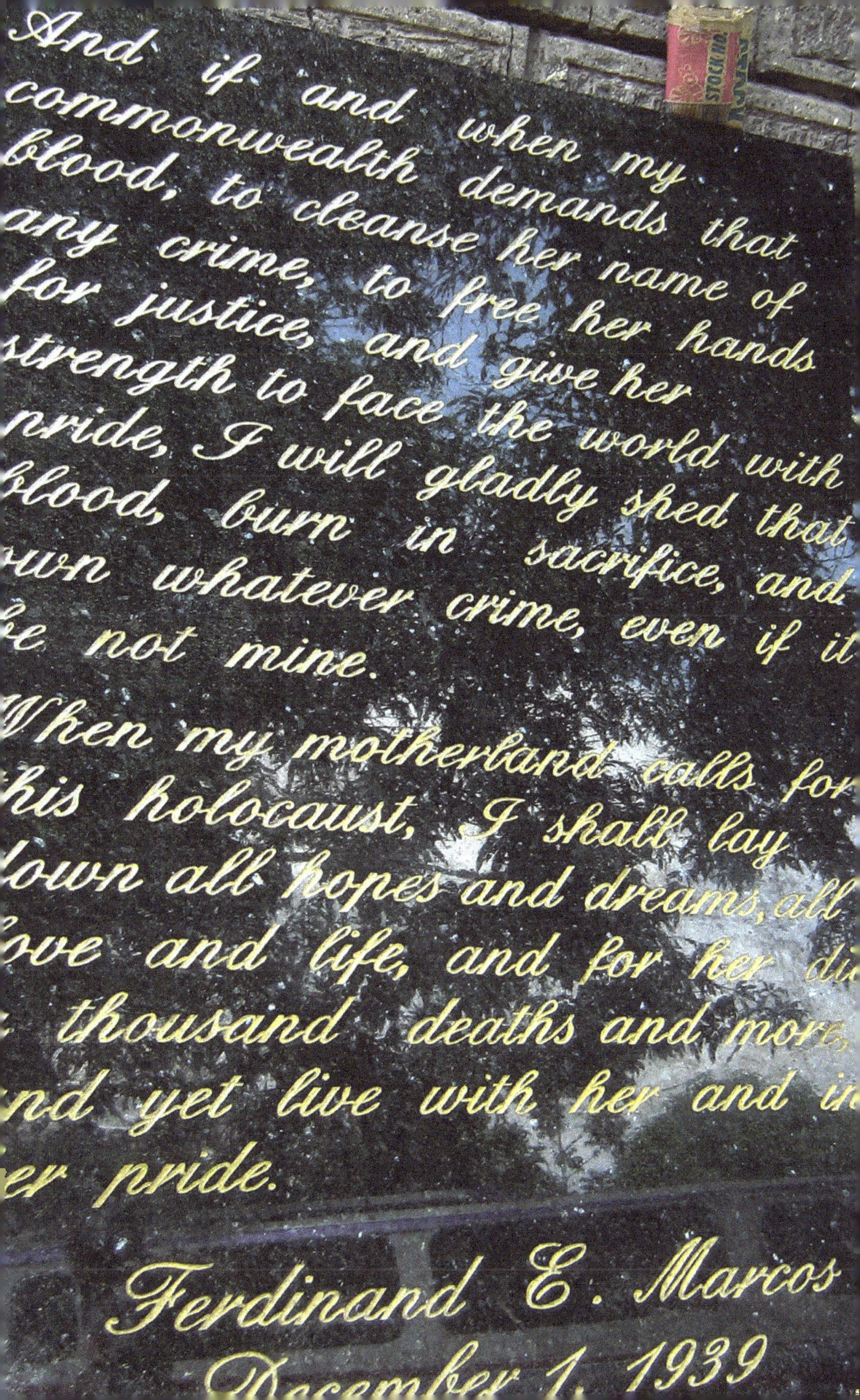

And if and when my
commonwealth demands that
blood, to cleanse her name of
any crime, to free her hands
for justice, and give her
strength to face the world with
pride, I will gladly shed that
blood, burn in sacrifice, and
own whatever crime, even if it
e not mine.

When my motherland calls for
his holocaust, I shall lay
lown all hopes and dreams, all
ove and life, and for her di
thousand deaths and more,
nd yet live with her and i
er pride.

Ferdinand E. Marcos
December 1, 1939

# welcome home

For years and years, we kept on losing hope
to liars, crooks, and cheats who promised change.
They lead our lives toward a downward slope
where darkness reigned and left us fools of rage.

We witnessed laughter turn into despair
when running kids become a statistic.
They lie wide-eyed, with dreams beyond repair.
From counting sheep to body count. It's sick

how leaders sleep at ease while people grieve
and hope and grieve and hope. We're stuck! In love
with self-proclaimed heroes and kings who live
and lead with make-believe fear— *never love.*

Some say that grief is love without a home.
Welcome home, Love, for years and years to come.

*opposite: gorjaz girlz – painting by ja amores*

# mga tanong na hindi ko inaasahang tanongin in this lifetime pero tinanong rin after may 9

1. Paano ko ba gagawing tungkol sa akin ang eleksyon na 'to?
2. Ilang oras ka pumila sa presinto?
3. Nasiraan din ba kayo
   ng machine?

4. Saan galing yung mga bilang na 'to?

5. Ano na mangyayari bukas?
6. Sa tingin mo ba magkaka-EDSA ulit?
   6.1. Kaya ba today?
7. Ano?! Kahapon pa kayo nakapila?
8. Punta ka bukas?
   8.1. Woke ka ba?

9. Uy ano sa tingin mo, kaya ba nating ituloy mga events?
   9.1. Pwede pa kaya tayo mag gig?

10. Ano nang gagawin ko?
    10.1. Makakahanap kaya ako ng tapang at lakas
    para magsulat?
    10.2. O pipikit na lang ako at magsasaya habang nalulungkot
    ang lahat?
11. Paano ulit mag-private ng profile?
12. Kung sakali lang... anong gagawin namin kung na-red tag kami?
13. Magkano bayad sa DDS troll? PHP2.5M?
    13.1. Mapapatawad ba yung nangonsensya?
14. Saang bakery tayo magkikita?

15. Safe pa ba magsuot ng pink?
16. What should I wear to a protest? A napkin, a tampon or a cup?
17. Ano meaning ng mang dodogshow?
18. Dapat bang kaibiganin pa rin ang mga taong iba ang paniniwala sa atin?
    18.1. Paano tayo makikipagintindihan
    kapag tayo'y nagbibingi-bingian?
19. Ba't niyo kinakausap sarili niyo?
    19.1. Are you a nurse din po?

20. Paano tayo magkaka-empatiya sa mga naloko at naniniwala sa kasinungalingan?

21. 'Yan ba yung nawawalang Picasso painting… sa likod ni tita Meldy?
22. What's wrong with taking a trip to Australia?
23. Sino may contact na lawyer in case of emergency?
24. Paano mag-preserve ng mga libro at sine?
25. Paano maging double major?
26. Need pa bang picturan?
27. Choco na gatas o gatas
    nga ba katapat ng tear gas? Tubig ba?
    27.1. Contacts o salamin?
28. Bakit? Sinong nag red-tag sa inyo?
29. May tips po ba kayo
    kung sakaling mahuli ako?
    29.1. Ano yung isisigaw ko
          kung mahuli ako?

30. Ano pa ba ang pwedeng gawin maliban sa pag-protesta?
31. Paano ulit mabubuo itong watak-watak na archipelago?
32. Anong masama sa paghihingi ng hustisya at mabuting kinabukasan?
33. *Mi patria adorada*, hanggang ganito na lang ba talaga tayo?

# questions i never thought we'd have to ask in this lifetime but were asked after may 9, 2022

1. Hmm... how do I make the elections about me?
2. How many hours did you line up at the precinct?
3. Did your voting machine break down as well?

4. Where did these numbers come from?

5. What's going to happen tomorrow?
6. Will there be an EDSA Revolution again?
    6.1. Do you think it's any time soon?
7. What?! You've been in line since yesterday?
8. Are you coming to the protest tomorrow?
    8.1. Oh, you're woke?

9. Hey guys, in light of current events, do you think we'd still be able to push through with our event this weekend?

9.1. Can we still book gigs?

10. What should I do now?
    10.1. Will I still have the strength and courage to write?
    10.2. Or will I just let myself live the bliss of office hours?
11. How do we set Facebook profiles to private again?
12. Theoretically... what do we do if we ever get red-tagged?
13. What? How much was the online troll paid? PHP2.5M?
14. Which bakery will we meet at?

15. Is it safe to wear pink?
16. What should I wear to a protest?    A napkin, a tampon or a cup?
17. What does it mean to "dogshow"?
18. Should we still befriend those who have different beliefs as we do?
    18.1. How do we find common ground?
    18.2. Is there any left to begin with?
19. Why are you talking to yourselves?
    19.1. Are you a nurse din *po?*

20. How do we have empathy for those who believed in lies in hopes for better lives?
21. Is that... The lost Picasso painting behind Imelda?
22. What's wrong with taking a trip to Australia?
23. Who has a lawyer we can contact in case of emergencies?
24. How do we preserve movies and books?

25. How does one become a double major?
26. Do you really have to take a picture at a graduation?
27. Milk or water? To wash tear gas?
    27.1. On that note, should I wear glasses or contacts?
28. Why? Who red-tagged you?
29. Do you have any tips in case I get caught?
    29.1. What am I supposed to shout if that happens?

30. Is there anything else we can do beyond protesting?
31. How can we bridge this divided and conquered archipelago?
32. Is it wrong to ask for justice and a better future?
33. *Mi patria adorada,* are we going to stay like this forever?

# ang dami nanamang bilihin!

Taon-taon na lang namimili!

Paulit-ulit na pinuno
ng barya ang baboy na hingi nang hingi
taon-taon na lang! Namimili
ngunit namamali sa pagbabahagi ng utang
na loob na hindi mabuo-buo.

Taon-taon na lang namimili.
Paulit-ulit na pinuno.

i can no longer afford
to care. words are my currency
& i have Nothing left
to say. this is not the first time
a woman gracefully put down
her pride for a child
who wants to be king of the world.

i've lived this story
a thousand times & see it coming
a thousand more
i'll save my words.
everything's been said
yet, Nothing done.

# corpse pose

*When you're ready, go ahead*
*and lie down*
*flat on the floor.*
*Spread your arms*
*by your side*
*Stretch your legs*
*like sunlight at dawn.*
*Draw the navel down*
*to the ground. Rest your back*
*into the earth.*
*If it's safe to do so,*
*close your eyes*
*and breathe.*
*Shavasana.*

*A surrender.*

*Take a deeeeep deep breath in*

I take in the stormy weather outside,
finding stillness
from within. Trying
not to listen
to the trees whipping
from a distance,
and my mother's footsteps
walking from the kitchen
as she turns on the television
to watch the news.

*Take another inhale*

I'm sinking to relaxation, thinking
of not thinking
about the war
between two nations
I never really cared for.
Missiles flying over countries.
The upcoming elections.
Political decisions in abortions.

*opposite: real world – digital manipulation by pam*

The inevitable price hikes
of gas, and ultimately
everything else.

Wow. All that and
here I am just
lying on the floor.

Is it rude to find peace
amidst bullets
of uncooked rice
clanging on metal?
Blood, sweat, and tears dripping,
from my mother's skin. Her thumb
instead of an onion. She is thrilled.
The piercing screams
of a boiling kettle.
The sizzling fire fueling
tiny explosions
of oil being poured on a pan.
The power-hungry
stirring the pot
of hot soup for four.

*Take the deepest breath*
*you've taken today*
*for four, three, two...*

I never knew war could smell
like sautéed garlic and onions;
that dinner could sound
like battle troops burning
bridges to cut food supply lines.

I lie there fighting
my hunger and wonder:
how much will a can of Spam cost tomorrow?
*No. I don't wanna know.*

As I inhale, I float
like a cartoon character
following the aroma
of an iron-hearty, very healthy
combat soup
for the soul.

I open my eyes,
and finally
                    *exhale.*

Dinner is served.
We eat
        in news fatigues.
I wash the dishes.

# kasaysayan ng katawang-lupa

Ako'y naging isang arkipelago.
napaliligiran ng sariling luha–
na siyang bukod-tanging monopolyong
mananatiling *akin* habang sila'y
sakop nang sakop nang sakop
sa aking katawan, yaman, at pagmamahal.
Ako'y bininyagang banal na birhen;
dinakip at ginahasa;
inalipusta't inalipin;
nalulunod sa sariling dagat.

Nilusob nila ang aking dalampasigan
bawat isla ko'y pinagpapasa-pasahan
sa kagalanggalangang lalaking
manlulupig.
kada braso't binti'y
tinadtad, inangkin, pinagwatak-
watak para sa makasariling luho.
Ako'y nandirigma
laban sa sarili: aking kanang kama'y
hindi kinikilala ang dugo ng kaliwa.
Sila'y may kanikanilang diyos mula
sa magkakasalungat na langit.

Wala na akong magagawa kundi umiyak–
punitin ang kasarinlan: isang batang
binansagang Inang Bayan, inaalay ko
ang sarili ko– ako'y luluhod, ako'y
dudugo at magdadalang
pitong libong anak.
Ipagkakalat sa dagat nang mailuksa
ang pinagnasaang paraisong
pinaubaya sa kahapon.

# geohistory of body

I have become an archipelago.
I surround myself with tears.
It's all I can monopolize
for myself while everyone keeps
taking & taking & taking
my body, my money, my love.
My heart is submerged.
I'm baptized & holy.
I'm invaded & assaulted.
I'm pilfered & a subject,
drowning in my own skin.

They come inside
my open shores
for men to govern
my every island. Each limb
divided & conquered, pulled
apart for their selfish comforts. I'm at war
with myself: the north does not pray
with the south, their gods
are from quarreling heavens

& all I can muster is
cry–
tear away my skin,
my unwilling womb, I offer
myself on my
knees: pleading,
bleeding & birthing.
My seven thousands
scatter
to sea & mourn
the rich paradises
I could have been.

Pam Concepcion

# stripping down

When you strip yourself
from namesake to naked skin
where does human stop?



*opposite: stripped to a degree – watercolor by pam*

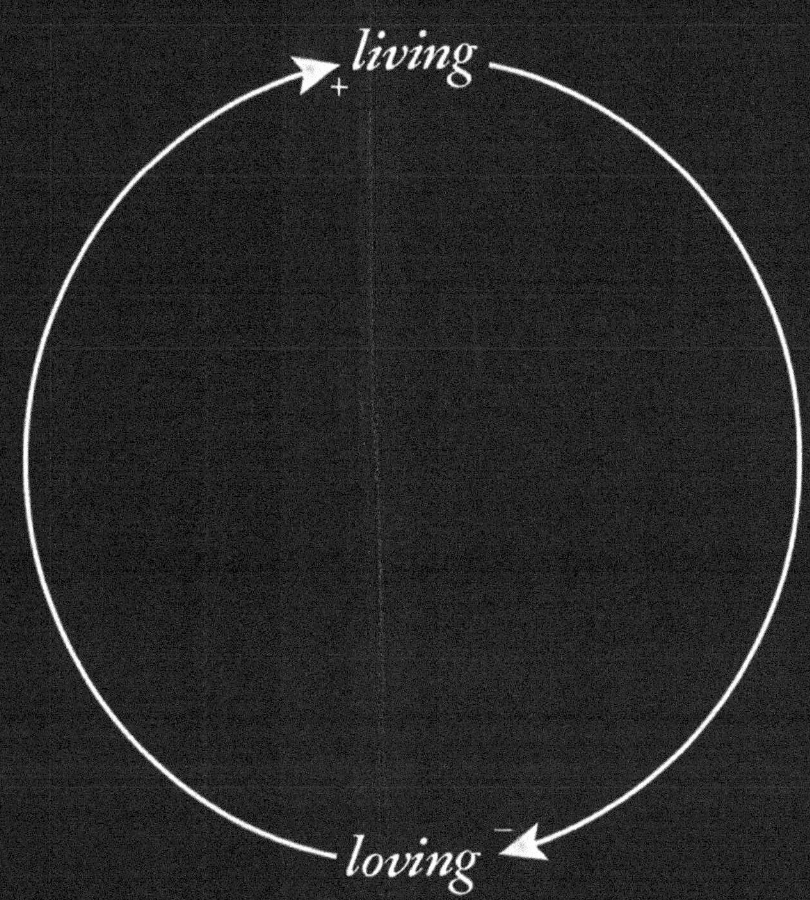
living
+
loving
−

# love & late-stage capitalism

*Not right now, love.*
*We're too tired to love.*
We just entered
the working force.

It terrified me before
just thinking about
*"Where do I see myself*
*in the next five years?"*
When I see my sister,
and childhood friends
less and less regularly,
like our periods–

We all have PCOS now.
It's as if our bodies
are telling us
*this* is not a regular
pace to live at.

What was once a time
for afternoon runs
and after-school trainings
was now after work traffic.

Shifting passions to hobbies
and retrospection
in the name of practicality?

I've gotten a glimpse
of this life myself
while learning to be a leader in:
*"innovation, research, entrepreneurship, and nation-building"*
in other words, college.

I had a five-year plan
of building my own
little nation of stability:
studying decision-making
and the trade-offs
that will inevitably occur

if I lay foundations first
before I love Full Time–*allthetime.*

I learned the more I wanted to excel
in optimizing industries,
the less time I have
to wash my hair
and write this poem.

Would my teachers think I made
the most profitable decision
when they see me
with the healthiest curls
I've had my whole life
while I read this poem?

I've now left home, looking
for part-time jobs
like teaching kids
or brewing coffee
so I can still love on the side.
Instead, I found an espresso shot
of love from a man who always holds me
like he loves me
but couldn't find
the optimal schedule in his life
to love me the way
I should be loved.

My friend said everyone in LA
is just too obsessed with stability.

*Tell me, love,*
*why do we keep loving*
*in the realms of rationality?*

Back home, my sister found you too, *love,*
gifted through coffee beans, gin and tonic
with notes of magic,
but they were just *too busy*
with what The Businessman
Who Owns The Stars called *"matters of consequences"*
that I, too, am now busy with
in hopes of living

on my own
so I can regularly wash my hair,
and peacefully work
on the poems
I've been thinking&thinking&thinking about
but never having the time
to write them down.

As I mastered my trade, I learned
that the trade-off for stability
is our inability                                        to love.

# the power of habit (reprise)

*Oh, muscle memory routine!*
You set me free from all thinking
I'm in *love!*
with the four-wall safety
you contain me: mind, void
of emotion; legs always
in motion– constant
fluctuations promise
comfort predictions.
All expectations gain
satisfaction from serotonin
sensations of ticking boxes
off my daylist, yet
the body recalls rest
from playfield days.
I keep leaving
cracks in this habit hideout
only to find out
these rabbit holes I crawl toward
are breathing spaces to fall in
love! with life. *again..*

*opposite: shapes of stagnation – digital art by pam*

## i hate love poems

i just wanna be
those rebellious Punk poets shouting
raw and unpolished verses
in dissonant singing

~~I AM AN ANTI CHRIST~~
beating on the brat
with a baseball bat
we're going straight to hell
rock and roll
the loss of control,
unfocused shots of
wrecking guitars
tattoos piercings ripped jeans spiked hair&
worn out shirts screaming
~~(A)~~NARCHY

i wrote about politicians
& their Sexist jokes
on the correlation between
beautiful women and rape
& letting the mayor go first.
education systems
getting a Hard-on
for Profit over people

for Profit over people
conditioned to serve
the Global Supply Chain
of fashion & trash production
spewing out engineered images
that make me hate myself

then I grew tired
of hate—
and being angry.

So, I started writing
about you, sitting
beside me,
amidst all chaos,
watching me type
this poem
on my phone
as you take a sip
from my coffee mug.

You used to spit out black coffee.
Now it's all you can drink.
I used to hate love poems.
Now it's all I can write.

# real world self-care checklist

- □ hand-washing my underwear on a sunday morning
- □ detangling my hair once a week
- □ scheduling my payments
- □ setting that doctor's appointment
- □ changing my beddings
- □ stretching my calves and hamstrings
- □ cleaning my room
- □ strengthening my arms despite instilled insecurities
- □ making plans with myself
- □ making plans with friends
- □ pushing through with said plans
- □ calling off work when I'm sick
- □ saying I'm not fine when I'm not fine
- □ listening to my friends' voice recorded chisme at work
- □ reviewing my expenses every two months
- □ watching the videos my friends send me
- □ taking inventory of my emotions
- □ letting my hair down instead of a bun
- □ packing my lunch the night before work
- □ showing up to that doctor's appointment
- □ looking for a new job
- □ letting myself be angry when I'm angry
- □ putting my newly washed clothes in the closet
- □ setting aside money for savings
- □ investing in myself
- □ remembering to put lotion on
- □ sleeping before midnight
- □ closing all my mental and digital tabs
- □ replying to messages I've been avoiding
- □ remembering to breathe
- □ facing the thoughts and feelings I've been avoiding
- □ crying while watching 5cm Per Second for the nth time
- □ leaving my vape at home
- □ stopping everything I'm doing to eat on time
- □ eating without brain rotting on the phone
- □ eating properly, sitting down at a table
- □ washing the dishes
- □ thanking everyone
- □ revising my drafts
- □ turning down booty calls
- □ reading a book on the train

- ☐ staring at the ceiling while listening to music
- ☐ keeping my screen time below 5 hours
- ☐ watching that movie a friend told me to watch
- ☐ putting on make-up at home and not on the train
- ☐ planning tomorrow's outfit
- ☐ imagining the day ahead
- ☐ applying eyeshadow and eyeliner like a renaissance painter
- ☐ cooking dinner for my family
- ☐ posting my art online
- ☐ sitting in silence with my private transit system of thoughts
- ☐ maintaining relationships with friends
- ☐ accepting what I don't and can't know right now
- ☐ learning how to be
- ☐ making an effort &
- ☐ carving out the space to love

# ode to pop punk

I keep thinking maybe I suck at love
I'm addicted; I'd do anything:
I always have the time to listen to you
whine. A bouquet of clumsy words,
a simple melody; a song that never stuck

at first but I grew to like. We would drink
too much & talk about god– I promise
I'll go to church on Sunday so please
go with me on Friday night. I'll MakeDamnSure
to be California's best. I'll dream

another sunset with you, stagger home
after midnight & somehow everything's gonna fall
right into place. Time will fly like a dove &
all the small things will feel like
a slow dance on the inside. I'll wake up
with the fondest memories, while you're good to go &

going nowhere fast. Your foot is out the door
you said "I don't love you
like I did yesterday."
I cannot speak; I've lost my voice; speechless
& redundant cause *I love you's* not enough–
my mind played tricks on me.

We are an example of why not to fall in love;
all these English Girls & American Boys just like sex;
you're a fever I can't sweat out & who I think about in bed.
Yet I'm trying to forget I'm addicted– I can't keep my hands off
you. I know I'll survive, so I'd do anything
to dive right back into you cause no one
breaks my heart like you.

# what's so scary about dinner?

I've yet to meet a man
who doesn't flinch
at the question:
*Can we have dinner first?*

After mindless minutes of downloading
digital daydreams, uninterrupted back and forths,
Pavlovian responses to pocketed vibrations,
frustrated fingers tap tap tapping on the qwerty,
the query sends
them in theories of meaning.

*Can we have dinner first?*
A question somehow equating to
*It's a trap!*
*These females just want free meals!*
Well, I can feed myself fine every day, thank you!
But if you're too broke
then pay with your pride:
look me in the eye,
and ask me: *hey um, can we split the bill?*
or better yet: get paid first?

In other cases, it could also mean
*I want to date you* *seriously.*
Seriously? Did I say that?
Have you considered we haven't even met
beyond this 6" crystal display? Do tell me...
*Gago, sino ka ba?*
to lock the door behind me
before I've held your hand
or caught your cologne?

I just need witnesses and alibis
in the form of a bartender or a server
taking our orders, on top of
live-location sharing with my friends.

Does every man think like this?
Is it the law?
If so, who wrote these rules
and passed them down
without so much as a tease or a G&T? So

*No.*
I'm not gonna fuck      on an empty stomach–
I'm acidic.
I don't want to ramble and rumble
as we fumble our way to bed.

I'm the writer here.
I'll be the one to marinate meaning into my words.

When I say: *"Can you please take me out somewhere first?"*
I mean read my free recipe for the best Dinner Date
that *could* organically cook up a hook up:
prep the ingredients
dress up nice,
insist on picking me up,
        (despite the back and forth)
sauté me with your smiles and eyes
as I cartoonishly float to the aroma
of your woody, musky fragrance.
Slow-cook the moment while we
carefully choose conversations.
Make me want you      with your food
for thought. Let me savor
the smell of cooking
before I eat it

Then, *maybe,*
you can have me.

# contraction of heavenly bodies

I hate this unlarge body of mine
that I've religiously fed
to contain my multitudes.

All I see are eyes
averting the soul
only to trace curves
of the exterior.

I'm slowly getting tired of shrinking
this already tiny vessel.
I'm close to imploding
the vastness of my mind
& remain uncharted, unheard, & unseen.

All I can do is strip
& break away the shell
of the tangible self, destroy
distractions of skin touching skin,
constraining my inner universe
from expanding            infinitely.

# spring awakening

It was my first date ever
in this city
I            never quite liked,
but I haven't been here
in the springtime before.

You gave me a pink pot of pink flowers
that live longer than expensive bouquets.
We drove past roads invaded
by yellow flowers looking like stars
on a sky of green leaves.

I've only been here four months
but I've already grown
tired. This country of excess–
so obsessed with extra-large fast-food servings,
twenty-four-hour news cycles
multi-lane freeways,
& extra fast cars– it fueled
my indifference
to the abundance
of those wild mustard flowers
that took your breath away.

You stopped driving to say:
*Wow, isn't that beautiful?*
It was *my* first time here, not yours
yet, your eyes had more wonder than mine.

We sat under the shade of a tree.
You brought me champagne, prosciutto, & brie,
but I mostly just ate the grapes & green mangoes–
*I'm sorry I was nervous.*

You were asking me things
no one's ever asked me,
listening as I go back
to four years ago
where the mangoes
were sweet & yellow,
& the beaches,

like the flowers you gave—
know no season.
Always warm,
always in bloom.

The sun back home was different.
It never burned me
the way this SoCal sun
always threatened to start
a brush fire
on this bushy
head of hair,
& dries my clay
colored skin
to a cracked drought.

One day, I tried to run,
when the leaves have eaten up
the warm orange of the sun.
The sky giving us cold
shoulders hidden
beneath layers of clothes—
I was under the weather for a week.

But that day in the park,
the flowers bloomed
in colors I never see at home.
The sun shone
in your eyes the way mine did
at home.
I can finally see
how this city can          grow
on me.

It's been a while since then—
I've swam on cold beaches.
I've ran without the sun.
I've planted my roots.

The flowers you gave are still alive
with hopes that I bloom, then
blossom as bold
& bright
as you.

*pages 104-105: loss 4 words – digital manipulation by pam*

No. ..........................

DATE 4 / 21 / 23

~~I'm a writer~~

~~weaving them wrecking walls~~
~~with words;~~
~~walking the walls wounds~~
~~with words~~

I said I'll write you
but you left me at a loss
for words to finish

I said I'll write you
but you left me at a loss
for words to finish

saying less, I'm
losing a lot of words

I tried to write you
but you left me at a loss
for words to finish

~~weaving words to wreck the walls~~
~~walking words to walk the wounds~~

i tried to write poems
on a page but
i am a writer
but now you have me
at a loss for words

i wanted to write
but you had me at a loss
for words to write

i wanted to write
but you left me at a loss
for words to finish

* napakahalagang
pag-iingat nang ko
ying mga solitary
kakitaan ko.

silence vs. speaking

No.

DATE / /

a writer but you had me at a loss for words
wasn't half the things you said i was
in years ago
economy of words is at a recession
what if i put all my words in a time deposit
to the point where i can no longer speak
unless necessary? and the words i will
speak will have never been
voiced, never rang truer, never forgotten,
but always remembered?

DATE 4 / 21 / 23

i have put up a time deposit
in my personal word bank
these carefully crafted words
to remain unspoken for years
until i am of age to do so
and when spoken, i will yield
a rich return on investment
not for me, the speaker of the words
but for the recipients of them.
many times [illegible] today
[illegible]
is the date of [illegible]

saying less, i'm
[illegible] a lot of words

# foundations

*(Prologue to Siege)*
*

In narrative structures,
a siege is when an external force
comes without invitation:
*an invasion.*

In physics,
an object is said to remain at rest
or moving in constant velocity
unless acted upon by an external force.
*The first law of motion.*

In screenwriting,
routines are built
into several scenes,
just to be broken
by one.
*A disruption.*

In consumer behavior,
people don't notice
buying habits transition
as we transition
to a new sequence in life,
like a graduation or a new relationship.
To us, it's growth; but to retailers?
*Market penetration.*
*

Phenomenon of seemingly disconnected
origins that share one oscillation,
one behavior over time graph:
foundations of the human condition.

# siege

Every day, I wake up at seven
to get up at eight and meditate away
last night's nightmare of
falling
in love with someone
I used to love,
missing deadlines, losing teeth,
or running
from civil unrest that
rendered me restless—
craving for a cup
of confidence:
freshly hand-ground
then hand-poured,
dripping a deep chestnut color,
waking me up
for a second time then I

eat breakfast before I
walk my dogs before I
work out before I
shower before I
work before I
eat lunch before I
work again before I
watch the news before I
eat dinner before I
shower again before I
doomscroll before I
sleep before I

I woke up at eight before

I got up at nine to meditate away

last night's dream

of falling

in love with someone new.

I brewed a cup of

tea,

calming me down then

I eat breakfast

I walk my dogs

I work out

I shower

I work

I eat lunch

I work through a daydream

I watch Gilmore Girls

I eat dinner

I shower again

I read and write poetry

I–

I deliberately built walls
of repetitive motions
for the notion of stabilization.
Safe from commotions
and unexpected explosions
of emotions I have kept
in constant slow motion.
Safe from the civil unrest
that renders me restless at night
but not from invasions
of external forces.

The walls have begun cracking,
leaving spaces and openings
in between hours,
for me to be besieged
by thoughts
of you.

---

Now that you're here, I'd like to ask:
Am I also the siege that conquered
your mind the same way you've invaded
my thoughts and disrupted
my days?

Did you wake up
an hour later than your alarm?
Did you take a new route
on your morning run?
Or was it on your commute?
Did you buy a brand of butter
different from what your mother would buy?
Did you dream of an old lover
then dream of another?
Did you brew tea instead of coffee too?
Did you burn your tongue while drinking it
as I crossed the borders of your mind?

Were you restless
like a chain-smoker an hour after
their last drag? Reaching
for your pocket
to check your phone
for the second time
in the last five minutes,
in hopes of something– anything
like the slightest hint of interaction
brought upon by tiny hearts floating
on your screen, making us
a few degrees closer
than we were
two minutes ago.

Or is this just an invasion
conjured by my imagination?
Am I waging war
under the first law of motion
or the third?
Did I just let myself get pushed
off the top of a hill, stuck
in a constant free fall on my own?
Are you still plotting reactions– retaliations
toward my direction?

If so, will you please sign
this peace treaty with me,
so we can transition
to that sequence where
we're two sovereign bodies
buying an English tea set
and a French-press
for when we visit
each other's places?

# complementary blending

I saw you across the room
at the other end of the spectrum.
I didn't know who you were
nor have I met anyone else
who has the same hue as you.

Yet you strode to where I stood
and filled me with bold strokes
in the form of complimentary
drinks and compliments
with a wink that made me think
if you saw my cheeks blush pink,
then flush two shades darker.

We hatched words
in the negative spaces
between our bodies,
hands brushing lightly,
skin grazing against skin,
arms holding each other tightly.

You were green while I was pink.
From another angle, we make ninety.
We're bittersweet.
We're sugar and spice.
Our bodies blended
colors and flavors,
our friends wouldn't know
who's who,
or whose hue was whose.

Our bodies were bold
strokes of lovers on each other
with strokes of old others on each lover.
No matter how much I
trace my fingers around them,
stipple my lips against them,
graze my tongue over them,
their taste and traces remain.

I guess lovers always leave
a mark, but I thank them
for leaving you.
So, I too can find new spots
to stroke as proof
that I was here
at least once...

or twice more,
now with pressure,
now with pleasure,
working on the part
I had left earlier.
Brushing wet paint
on slightly wet paint–
blending my color unto you
and yours                    unto me.

*inspired by a Melodie Perrault painting*

# indulgence

Let me indulge in you
& bask in your waking whispers
sunrising their way into
the silence of my dream world.
Blurred frequencies of an alarm & a lullaby;
adrenaline & adenosine arguing in my head:
*It's 4am but this is not my bed.*
Yet, these weightless lids & lashes
gave in to the gravity
of your voice:
*It's okay. You can sleep.*

Let me delight in you
while you brew two
morning mugs
of medium roast pour over
dosing on the words
that walk on our lips
exchanging secondhand
breaths & a buttery breadth
of stories for breakfast.

Let me invest in you
even if we're wound up
in our own little worlds of working.
We can meet up for lunch
in that hidden metaphysical spot
we always go to for
wondering        & thinking
of each other.

Let me revel in you
in the slowness of siesta hours
cut me up a line
of your cocaine kisses;
grant me all my champagne wishes;
add a bit more key bumps
on my blushing cheeks
for merienda

to make time move
a little faster
so we can move on
to dinner &

indulging in you—
all of you
al lover&over&overagain.

# 15-line sonnet for every floor before we reached the stars

I let parking lot apologies be-
come heated exchanges          of red lip tint.
I felt forgiveness flow right out of me
even when better halves say               I shouldn't.

But *you,* beside *me?* That's       all I wanted
along with that Mezcal mix please, while you
sing me this song of the unrequited.
Had we space    and time, we'd have danced    'til two,

and broke                    our elevator     to the stars
like a time machine stuck in the moment
looping, repeating, rewinding the part
where our lips sparked– overloading currents,

blacking out     my words to write this sonnet
replaying like reels on the internet,
wishing            to overwrite time beyond it.

# shorthanded

I wish we could spend
more time, but the shorthand counts
in hourly wages

# magic sing

Mahal, okay lang ba
kung gaya ng kanta'y
minsan lang kita iibigin?
Hulog-hulog lang ng singko
sa KTV kung kailan kaya ko.

Salit-salit tayo:
sa tig tatatlo't kalahating minuto,
hangga't maubos ang inipong
barya sa alkansyang bote
ng alak na muntikan kong masagi
noong una mo akong hinagkan.

Mahal, okay lang ba?
Pagkasyahin muna natin 'tong crispy sisig
Na mamaya'y mapababayaang kumunat?

Salit-salit tayo:
isa kakanta, isa taga bugaw ng langaw sa sisig
at sa katapusa'y paghahatia't
ipapatapaw at kinabukasa'y pananghalian
kakainin habang kinukuwento
sa mga kaibigan ang lahat
ng nangyari kagabi.

Mahal, pinapangako ko sayo:
makakaraos tayo sa'ting pagsasamang
tigsisingkong oras kada dalawang linggo
na mas bilang pa sa sahod ko.

i-Mamagic Sing ko lahat
ng problema natin para balang araw,
sabay-sabay tayo kakantang magadamag.

# comments from a poetry workshop

These poets were telling me
how great    I love
when    all I did was    write    a scene of lovers
guessing coffee roasts and flavor notes.

These poets they...    wished they could wear
my glasses–    the one you liked.
They said I made the world more beautiful
with every word I utter    but I don't think
I have    ever loved or been called
*beloved.*

So, what do I know about it?

Can we just...    get back to the workshop
and criticize meaning instead?    *Tell me I'm wrong about love.*
Disprove the truth beneath my words.
Debate my meaning of agape–
Shouldn't poets know all about this already?

These poets... they...    they don't know the first law
of thermodynamics.
My words were only written
to alter the love    I can't seem to destroy.
I keep you hidden in electric lines
with insulated metaphors,
storing my current in these    capacitors of verse
before my psyche's circuits overload.

If my love is as great as they say it is, then    *why?*
why are you only my muse?

# bad haircuts

In the moment it always felt
so thrilling, like I will come
out, a new woman: head up,
hair down, confident & proud.

Yet I keep coming home
in tears & ugliness;
covering mirrors;
hiding hair & heart–

I've been trying to find the one
who could get my hair right.
Gone to the strangest places,
had the most awkward phases,
only to convince myself
with someone else's mirror:
*"I like this. I can live with this."*

but when you took my hair
in your hands, brushed it
from ear to shoulder to
see my face, I knew
I've had my last bad haircut.

because with you, I always come
home feeling more & more
me & even more & more
beautiful every day.

# nomadic

It was when your hands travelled
from shoulder to waist;
nomadic at best

when your belly cozied
perfectly on mine
a partial solar eclipse
changing tides

when your head nestled
in the crook of my arm
finding home *at last.*

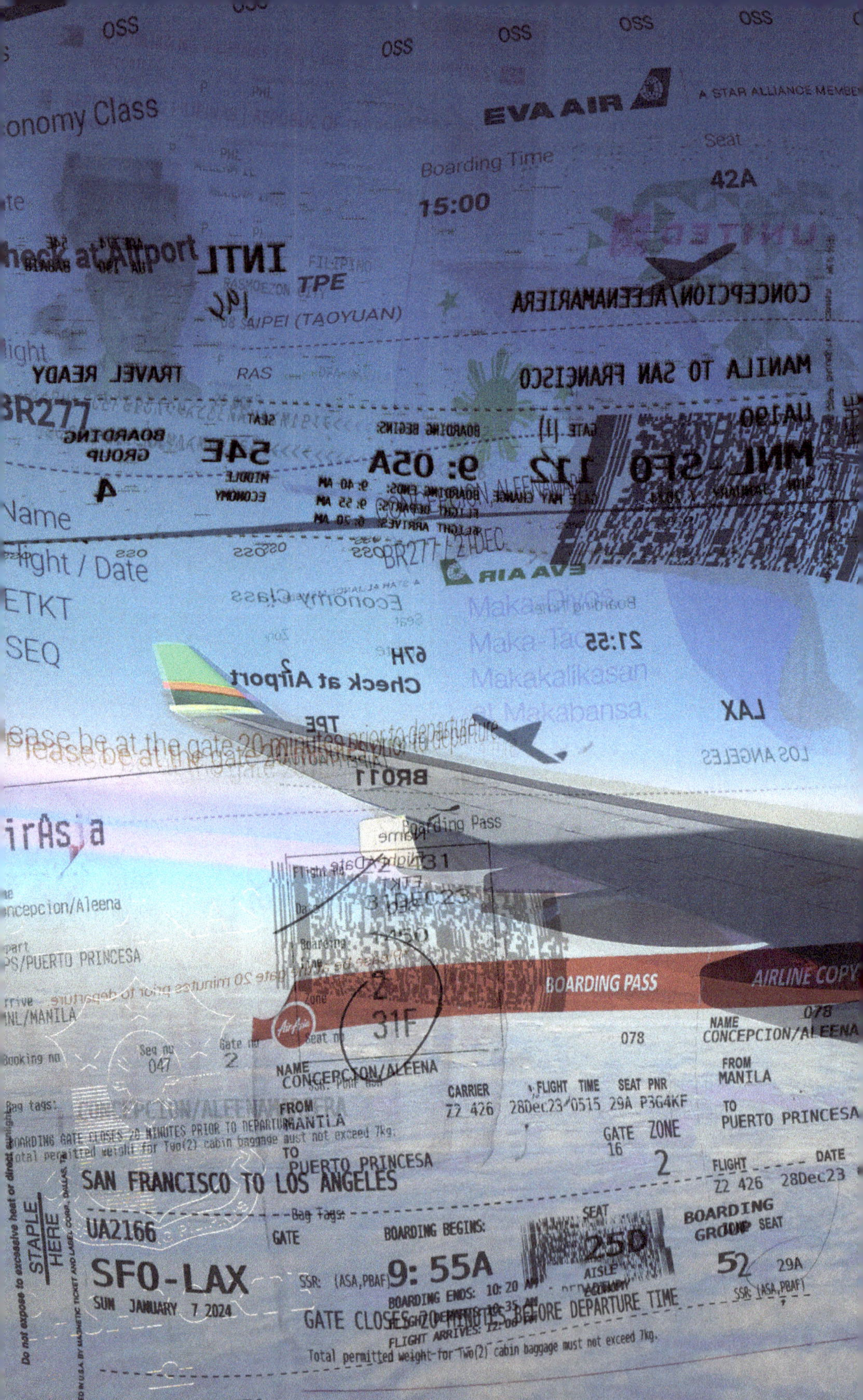

EVA AIR
A STAR ALLIANCE MEMBER
Economy Class
Boarding Time
15:00
Seat
42A
Check at Airport
INTL
TPE
TAIPEI (TAOYUAN)
BR277
Name
Flight / Date
ETKT
SEQ
Please be at the gate 20 minutes prior to departure
BR011
Boarding Pass
AirAsia
Concepcion/Aleena
PS/PUERTO PRINCESA
NL/MANILA
Booking no
Seq no
047
Gate no
2
Zone
2
Seat no
31F
BOARDING PASS
AIRLINE COPY
NAME
CONCEPCION/ALEENA
FROM
MANILA
TO
PUERTO PRINCESA
CARRIER
Z2 426
FLIGHT
28Dec23
TIME
0515
SEAT
29A
PNR
P3G4KF
GATE
16
ZONE
2
FLIGHT
Z2 426
DATE
28Dec23
SEAT
29A
078
BOARDING GATE CLOSES 20 MINUTES PRIOR TO DEPARTURE
SAN FRANCISCO TO LOS ANGELES
UA2166
SFO-LAX
SUN JANUARY 7 2024
GATE
BOARDING BEGINS:
9:55A
SEAT
25D
AISLE
BOARDING GROUP
5
GATE CLOSES 20 MINUTES BEFORE DEPARTURE TIME
Total permitted weight for Two(2) cabin baggage must not exceed 7kg.
STAPLE HERE
Do not expose to excessive heat or direct sunlight

# pag-uwi[5]

*Maraming beses na kitang nilayasan*
*Iniwanan at ibang pinuntahan*
*Parang lalaking ang hirap talagang malimutan*
*Ikaw lamang ang aking laging binabalikan*

*Manila*
*I keep coming back to Manila*
*Simply no place like Manila*
*Manila, I'm coming home*

Manila, please wait for me.
I booked a palindrome
of flights wishing it departs
tomorrow.

I'm sorry it took so long. I got caught
in the cruel coldness of circumstance
despite my resistance, I compromised
loving for leaving and living
with my family
in an economy
where I can still write this poem and get angry
at thirty minutes of moving traffic—
not a two-hour standstill,
or a four-hour *sardinas* commute.

Manila, do you remember
how we romanticized America as a monolith,
that fits in a 24x18x24 box?
We thought The States smell like Ivory soap
clinging to imported clothes;
that it sounds like pop punk cymbals
crashing on every beat,
or hip-hop hi-hats sizzling on 2's and 4's.

---

[5] coming home

Manila, you will laugh knowing
how LA smells like smoke and urine like you–
the difference here is
the high confidence of drugs
announcing its presence in the air
instead of deep-fried fish balls and kerosene.

Manila, I may have taken your noise for granted.
LA sounds like constant cat-calling for justice          speeding siren after
siren after siren then silence     for sudden stolen souls.
Manila, you were mostly spitting curses amidst sputtering engines;
quiet hi's wide eyes, whistles, warnings and whispers for          *hustisya.* [6]
You're subtly disrespectful like that,
but you were also 4pm humidity and karaoke songs for broken-hearted
drunks living under the walkway connecting D-Jose and Recto station.

here is blatant;
here is loud;
here is excessive;
here is angry;

yet for some reason, America thinks you're more dangerous–
that you'll rob them blind.
So far, you've only robbed my phone twice, Manila
but you do the same to everyone's taxes.
Did they teach you that after English class?
Here, I'm getting robbed
of my dignity every day with every locked&loaded sidewalk greeting.

Manila, I wish I could stay with you.
Your danger is no stranger to me.
I can drunkenly navigate your streets
after late night gigs of indie bands, and Happy Thursdays;
staying far from motorcycles skirting sidewalks, snatching phones
but you've robbed me too much of my time
waiting in line to get off the next station of my life,

---

[6] justice

so I left
after New Years
and suddenly
It's my first Thanksgiving now– I know
I said it means nothing to me
but it's making me look for *family*
in names I only know
from boxes and inboxes;
from thoughtfully thrown monthly mailed magazines;
in faces I only see in holiday phases;
in those who only remember you in time
for a funeral, Manila,

when I was looking for
the ones who took a day off
to see me off before my flight;
the ones who will drive dark Friday hours
to pick me up at NAIA,
then drive three more hours
for a welcome home dinner;
the ones who are always waiting
for me to come back so

I booked a palindrome
of flights wishing it departs
from *you*

*Hinahanap-hanap kita Manila*
*Ang ingay mo'y 'kay sarap sa tenga*
*Mga jeepney mong nagliliparan*
*Mga lasengga mong nagkakantahan*
*Take me back in your arms my–*

Manila, this Christmas
I'm coming home.

# friend dates

Let's have brunch
I'll block off a day for you.
Let's catch up & check out
that place you saw on IG—
*it's near both of us, TYG!!!*

I'll have that viral experimental dish:
Bicol Express turned to pasta;
you'll get that fall off the bone pork Adobo.
Slow-cooked and tender like our love,
unending from graduations to
job applications— lets drink

to that one you want to quit but still waiting
for the right time to. I say *maybe*
*you're just making excuses*
*out of fear?* In your defense,
you say that's also why I'm still
single. I gently deflect and redirect
to the latest schoolmate gossip
on who's pregnant, engaged, a doctor,
a lawyer, a CPA, an influencer, or abroad.

We swap stories and dishes;
sip from each other's drink; laugh
loudly, boisterously, like we're back
ungracefully sitting on covered court floors
cross-legged in skirts,
panties peeking shamelessly
while complaining about our teachers
and cramming for today's exam.
The giant history book on one knee,
yellow pad notes on the other.

We have the fanciest feast:
Jamaican patties, tuna Samgak Kimbap
twister fries, Bistek rice,
Buko juice, iced tea, and a shared
overwhelming academic stress,

unaware that we haven't moved on
to desserts— it's almost four!
We're buzzed and blushed.
Time had passed. We never noticed, we never stopped...
*Look!*

How far we've come.

# crab

Okay. Hold on to me,
my darling crab.
We're still in the same
boiling world.
We've walked on sunburnt sand,
hand in hand,
burrowed under
shared safe holes,
& waved goodbye
through high tides.

I watched with awe
as you rode your surf
but when my point broke,
you clung to me &
never let go.

Go on,
keep holding on.
Tug at my bikini strings,
strip off my glory,
claw our way down
to where you crashed.

Did you forget
the weight of two is always
easier to drown than one?

# two years and i still don't trust LA

Mommy, I don't like it here.
I'm having a hard time
finding friends
who don't want to fuck me.

The boys just want my body
without the soft pillows of love:
convenient & casual,
easy & transactional
for their own selfish desires.

There's no one to cry to, Mom.
Everyone else is an empty shell
of their online selves; angrily
progressive on their phones, ready
to claw at semantic mistakes
but toothless & carefree offline–

I'm in kindergarten all over again
when my *friends* made me sit
on the opposite side of the table–
I can't be beside them
until I'm useful to them.

Maybe you were right, I'm *too kind.*
My first instinct is to wear their shoes;
it could get me in trouble. I didn't think
my kindness could be a knife
that fucks me from behind.

Or maybe           I was right
for never wanting to be
in a city I'm not born & raised in.
The mountains & freeways tower over me—
I'm so small, so lonely & oh so beautifully           *sad.*

Should I just           *go home now?*

# pillow shots of solitude

*Take the next exit & drop me off*
*the nearest train station.*
*I'll have my fun on my own.*

One glass of pinot grigio,
One gulf shrimp aglio olio.
Candlelit dinner by the bar;
listening to the music talk.

I kiss the mouth
of the wine glass.
I stand directly in front
of a giant oil painting.

I walk myself home.
My cheeks caressed
by the evening breeze
moonlight touches my hand.

My fingers run through
cotton, denim, lace,      skin
my body bathes
in a symphony of silence.

I find that love
isn't a person,
but a cocktail mix
of feeling and living
this body I inhabit.

# to my friends who are depressed & hurting

My dog bit me every time
I treated his infected itchy ears.
It felt like exorcising a stubborn little devil.
The vet said *if he's lashing out*
*in aggression, or hiding in isolation,*
*he might be in pain—*
So much that he forgets
the scent he snores beside
on loud thunderstorm nights.

Is this how you are when you're hurting:
stripped down to survival & devoid of trust?
I'm reaching out my hand for you to hold
but you think you're a prickly porcupine, a hermit crab,
a turtle in its shell, a sea urchin, a hibernating bear.
*I don't want to lash out & drag you down with me;*
*I deserve to be alone, so I don't hurt anyone again.*

My darling, how dare you
think yourself unworthy of love?
Don't you know, it aches my heart
to see you in pain? So *please,*
take my hand. Dig your nails in
if it keeps you from falling. My skin is thick
and my roots are firm. I can hold us down.

I may not know the depths of your pain,
but I sure know how my dog falls asleep to me
scratching his now silky-smooth beagle ears.

# rushing sleep

In the heat of siesta hours,
you fell asleep in my arms.
Sweat sticking skin to skin,
hair glued to your forehead,
eyebrows furrowed.

My dear, what has this cold
and cruel world done
to make you so tired?
That even in your sleep you're
*rushing,rushing,rushing*
to get to thenextbreath
before it balloons your belly—
*running,running,running*
to get to thenextdream
before it inspires your psyche.

Why don't we slow down
exhale and
stop time?

Come, find rest in me.
I'll calm the climate down
with my hand-weaved Anahaw fan.

I'll hold you tight.
We can sleep
through the night.

# ceteris paribus

*"You can measure love:*
*by how many times you fight,*
*forgive, and how many times*
*you say sorry"*[7]

*All else held constant*
A thought experiment
in economics, to simplify the world's
infinite interacting variables.
Comforting our fears
of the unknown.

*ceteris paribus*
like casting a spell,
isolating x and y
in a predictable bubble,
assuming certainty
to forecasts we hold so dearly.

*all else held constant*
when prices increase
demand decreases
when prices decrease
demand increases

all else held constant
When gas prices increase
will we go on less dates?
When inflation increases
will my power to buy
you gifts decrease?
When interest rates rise up
will you retain interest in me?
When rent prices skyrocket
will you have to work more hours?

---

[7] *from my late Economics professor*

When you work more hours
Will your debt go down?
When we get better jobs
can we finally fight less?

*Ceteris paribus*

Let's cast this spell for a night
I'll put all our *sorrys* in the bank.
Will our return on investment be enough
to forgive all our debts
of time to each other?

Let's isolate me and you
from the macro and micro
and if all else held constant,
will you be able to hold me constant?

# promissory note

We keep on loving
in installments. I'm sorry, I
can't give it in full. Can I
love you with words for now?

Please just give me:
<u>Two (2) Weeks</u>, I promise
I'll buy us more
time– can we take out
a loan for memories?
Do you have enough
for yourself? If not,
can you lend me

your hand for now? I promise
I'll lend you mine
when you need it.

# parallelisms in work & love (or lack thereof)

I see the value of having you
in my company,
but I don't think I have the capacity
to commit to caring for you
while you work for me.
So, let's just do this
unwritten transaction:
*I take what I want from you*
*you take what you need from me.*
*don't be sad. just come*
*in. do the work. go home.*

# what is meaningful work anyway?

So, what if my job only sells?
No mission, no vision, no agenda to push,
only products for profit. An honest exchange
of service for the security and stability of a paycheck.

Does meaning only come
when I make a living from an altruistic
American savior complex of
*"doing good for the community"*
at the minimum wage?
Would that feed me?

What if I'm happy being selfish
fulfilling my own hierarchy of needing
to be in a better place than I was?
You say I'm selling my soul,
well, watch me feed it fat everyday

with this boring ass desk job,
I can excessively eat in restaurants
without discreetly peeking
at my cash and whispering to a friend
*"Hey, can you spot me first?"*

I've graduated from counting coins
I found in ashtrays and piggy banks
for two-way trike and train trips,
upgrading to middle class tricks
of train&Uber mix for sweatless savings, safety & style;

I've overcome the anxiety of paying
with prayers at grocery counters;
I'm paying for rent, and I'd share even more
if it spares another fight between my parents.
I can point to any furniture in my room,
and proudly say *I bought that.*

I can funnel funds to my art—
my craft has only gotten better
after affording guilt-free
rest & relaxation;

I can dream of flying,
showing myself the world
on a magic carpet
I weaved on my own.

I can even dare to consider
buying the power to play
goddess and create life
on my own body clock—*finally*,

I can see myself
five years from now,
in a better place than I'm in today.

## home economics and living education

*after Tess Gallagher and my mother*

My mother, she passes down links
of recipes from her province, with word
of mouth modifications to match
our Metropolitan Manila mixed taste.

Before flying to the States, she left me
a grocery list that served
as my mental template,
& oral tradition wisdom:
"Veggies & fish are fresher & cheaper
at the wet market." "When you buy a whole
chicken, tell the butcher *pang tinola cut.*"
"Here's my card, it's a checking account."
I always kept count of the present
balance versus items in the grocery cart.

Her wisdom crosses borders;
I followed her from grocery to grocery
"Ralph's has great deals on good meat"
"99 Ranch has fresh seafood"
"Get the whole young chicken
at Vons or Trader Joe's"
She's my translator
for peso to dollar, kilos to pounds,
Tagalog to Chinese veggie names.
Here's my card. Money won't stop
our tenderness.

My mother, she hands me down knowledge
on knife angles to slice melons, Baguio beans,
& julienne carrots. She was still
cooking, hours before
her flight home to bury
her mother & somewhere
behind her was her daughter,
learning to see how it's done.

# theories of growth

Maybe the next time you see me
it will be at a bookstore.
My hair will be a lot shorter,
yours, a different color.
Our arms, covered in ink,
            & our eyes,        a little bit            *wiser.*

Maybe I'll have a driver's license,
& you'll have a new car
because you finally found
a bearable job that feeds
your starving art—
comic prints I stumble upon in the store
while I'm restocking my book.

Maybe by then, we'll be better— *calmer*
at our balancing act
of living            *& loving*            on a tightrope.
With eyes closed, we can manage
credit & friendships,
paychecks & pages.                        *I'll pray:*

Maybe when we grow older
time will be kinder.

# new year, same me

*After 'Bagong Taon, Isang Palindromo' by Vijae Alquisola*

The new year starts
with ashfall once again
I can't help but cloud fears
of being the same person. Last year,
I can no longer distinguish the ruins:
volcanic or man-made,
past or present,
it's all the same disaster
regressing to mere concepts.
I've gotten burned out
from finding a new light
in a world that's been burning up.
The fire has crossed the second degree–
I've felt all that I can ever feel
& all I can say is
*"I've been here"* before
The year finally ends. [8]

---

[8] & when it ends, we look back at what has passed

# retractions

My love, I hereby retract all these poems and letters
I wrote to you; the same way Rizal did
his subversive stories– *Noli Me Tangere*, he said.
We never intended to start a revolution.
I only wanted a change
in your heart and mind
to assimilate with me.
We meant every word written at the time being
but alas,            it is now the death of us.

I built this city of poems
to house our love,
but your foundations of truth
began to crumble– held
together by intimate white lies
instead of mortar and egg whites.
Through dust and rubble,
I found your soul
is a walled city
you never dared enter alone.

Your conquest recognized no bounds.
You took and took and took my love
to enrich your id, ego, and libido.
I mistook you for a hero.           You're so
           greedy, so capitalist, so *American*
for saving this lonely colony,
granting me faux sovereignty,
making me your Queen–
which only makes me a woman           on a pedestal
and therefore, to the colonizers' eye:
                                        *the most desirable subject to conquer.*

Yet, the Maria Clara in me still gravitates toward          *praying*
to the Patron Saint of Lost Souls
that you, my dear Prodigal Boy,
make your way back home                    to yourself
where you'll find this last poem standing
amidst the aftermaths of war.
Take this, my past love, as *mi último adiós.*

# degrees of softness

soft is my favorite plushie
catching heartbreak tears

organic cotton underwear soaking in gentle soap;
handwash only, squeeze gently, do not wring

my beagle's fur by his neck,
on his chubbiest fat roll

fluffing newly cooked jasmine rice
steaming hot in the rice cooker

the bleached part of your hair, delicately wavy
with last-minute curls like a passing thought

my tears sitting on my waterline
slowly freefalling to my jawline

my boobs, days before my period, so sensitive, so tender,
my heart would cry at the slightest thought of you

& your belly— it caused the global pillow market collapse
the moment my head hits skin

the shyest, smallest kiss before entanglements
the silence of facing realities

the indefinitely last embrace to uncertainty

a painfully soft & shaky whisper *i'm sorry*
so unbearable, so sad, yet so undeserving of

a gentle forgiveness, calmly birthed from
a graceful exhale of patience— the softest thing there is.

# on rationality

I'm sorry, dear, but we need to love
rationally or we will burn
the sheets that keep us
warm, as you hold me
constant in your arms.

In a memoir I once read,
the writer's mother said
I have to save
10% of myself from everyone–
be it lover or daughter,
so I don't declare bankruptcy
in the currency of love
when the markets collapse.
At the end of the day,
It's the only investment we have
against the divine hand
conducting this quarter's score

but my love, we are not gods
who yield the power to control worlds.
We're left          to simplify these
complexities of love. We
fold it in half
again and again
until it fits in the spaces
between our fingers
counting hours of sleep;
finding frameworks to follow–
reaching for perfection.

In theoretical ideals,
I would love you *Fulltime*
we won't need revolutions
on television;
no red skies, no picket signs;
just me and you, rich
in rapid eye motion; high
on fumes from painted poetry
of clear skies and tulip fields     but
our human capacities

cannot handle nature's uncertainties
so we paint by numbers

we minimize all what ifs
make up *realistic systems*
of standardized affection
in clear-cut carats and traditional I do's
mediating in the meaning making of
*I love you I love you I love you*

mass-produced like semantic satiety,
inflating its value until it loses
all buying power.
The real becomes ideal, thus unattainable.

So again, we split the bills
of love, adjust
for inflation
and propose:
a scaled-down practical love,
a workable affordable predictable biweekly love
in microdoses of 5 dark Friday hours $\pm\ \sigma$
in hopes of managing
this project timeline of living
in the moment,
and finding love
in pockets of time

like this poem: birthed
on a Monday lunch break with
last night's dinner,
California strawberries,
Cara Cara oranges and Fuji apples—
my sweet, sweet slices of life.

# waiting for my hair to air-dry after midnight

These fresh white walls are one shade lighter than the popcorn ceiling. / I keep finding proof of the terrible paint job on the edges where wall meets objects. / Maybe it's time to put up all those prints from years of gigs & art fairs but / I don't have a centerpiece corkboard yet. / Why does this feel *so surreal?* I was just home two weeks ago and now I'm here / Again / This is probably dry enough to sleep in– *No.* I don't want a headache or a flat head. I mean is it really bad or something grown-ups just said? / Oh my god./ That self-confessed drug lord is spilling revelations of police-coerced implications on vigilante executions. / I wonder why I keep getting nightmares of dystopian danger & civil unrest. Did I not dry my hair properly last time? / I need to sleep. I work early tomorrow. Next time, I'll shower an hour earlier. / My table is a mess. Am I self-obsessed to have brought these medals across oceans as a reminder of who I once was? / Wow, I haven't picked up this book since pre-pandemic college days. / Do I reply to him now or tomorrow? Hmm... / I'll sleep on it. / Can I? It's been four hours. / Nope. Still damp. I'll shake it out a bit more. / The air is saturating with color / I smell coconuts, mangoes, Shea butter, Gardenias, sunflowers, avocadoes & home / I have a garden in my hair. / My hand trails down from root to split-end. / *My god,* how long my hair has grown.

# notes/references

1. **learning environment:** the quote "Lagi akong nagbabakasakaling babalik ka, kung kaya't parati akong naghihintay sa hardin na ating pinagtatagpuan." is said by Maria Clara in Jose Rizal's Novel, *Noli Me Tangere*

2. **mga tanong na hindi ko inaasahang tanongin in this lifetime pero natanong after may 9:** "pipikit na lamang at magsasaya habang nalulungkot ang lahat" is a reference to the song *Indak* by Up Dharma Down

   *Mi patria adorada* is a line from the poem *Mi Último Adiós* by Jose Rizal

3. **corpse pose:** "Her thumb / instead of an onion. She is thrilled." references *Cut* by Sylvia Plath

4. **love & late-stage capitalism; on rationality:** "fulltime allthetime" is a line from the song *Fulltime (Part-time Allthetime)* by Fieh

5. **love & late-stage capitalism:** The Businessman Who Owns The Stars and "matters of consequences" is from *The Little Prince* by Antoine de Saint-Exupéry

6. **i hate love poems** references the songs: *Anarchy in The UK* by The Sex Pistols, *Beat on the Brat* by The Ramones, and *Straight to Hell* by The Clash

7. **ode to pop punk** pays homage to the songs: *You Suck at Love; Addicted; I'd Do Anything; I Can't Keep My Hands Off You* by Simple Plan. / *Basket Case; Church on Sunday; Redundant* by Green Day / *Going Away to College; After Midnight; All the Small Things* by blink-182 / *Dead on Arrival; Saturday* by Fall Out Boy / *Growing Up; English Girls* by The Maine / *MakeDamnSure; A Slowdance on the Inside* by Taking Back Sunday / *Jaime All Over* by Mayday Parade / *Hallelujah; Pool* by Paramore / *I Don't Love You* by My Chemical Romance / *Liquid Confidence* by You Me at Six / *A Fever You Can't Sweat Out (album), Lying is the Most Fun a Girl Can Have Without Taking Her Clothes Off* by Panic! At The Disco

8. **comments from a poetry workshop:** "I have ever loved or been called/ beloved." recalls *Late Fragment* by Raymond Carver

9. **pag-uwi**: the first two quoted verses are from the song *Manila* by Hotdog

10. **home economics and living education** is inspired by the poem *I Stop Writing The Poem* by Tess Gallagher

11. **note on retractions:** Jose Rizal's retraction of his revolutionary work is a debated topic in Philippine History. Regardless of its veracity, the impact of his work still stands.

12. **on rationality:** "I have to save 10% of myself" is from memoir *Crying in H-Mart* by Michelle Zauner

13. **on rationality** also references the following songs: *Fulltime (Part-time Allthetime)* by Fieh; *The Revolution Will Not be Televised* by Gil Scott-Heron; *Feet Don't Fail Me Now* by Joy Crookes

# previously published

1. An older version of *laro lang* is part of a four-piece series *Pagdadalaga,* is published under De La Salle University's *Malate Literary Folio Tomo XXXVII Bilang 1 (2021).*

2. An older version of *relaxing* is published under De La Salle University's *Malate Literary Folio Tomo XXXVII Special Folio: Larawan ng Kasalukuyan (2021)*

3. *field of dreams* is published under De La Salle University's *Malate Literary Folio Tomo XXXVII Bilang 2 (2022).*

4. *field of dreams* was awarded the Best Literary Piece in Poetry for the Academic Year 2020-2021 in Gawad Midya 2023, the university's award-giving body for their Student Media Offices.

5. *field of dreams* is also published under Mama's Press Kitchen's sports anthology *Shooting Stars at Sky (2025)*

6. An older version of *menarche* is part of a four-piece series *Pagdadalaga,* published under De La Salle University's Malate Literary Folio Tomo XXXVII Bilang 1 (2021).

7. An older version of *kaibigan lang* is part of a four-piece series *pagdadalaga,* published under De La Salle University's *Malate Literary Folio Tomo XXXVII Bilang 1 (2021).*

8. An older version of *babaeng babae* is part of a four-piece series *Pagdadalaga,* published under De La Salle University's *Malate Literary Folio Tomo XXXVII Bilang 1 (2021).*

9. *2020+1 tokyo olympics* is published under Mama's Press Kitchen's sports anthology *Shooting Stars at Sky* (2025)

10. An older version of *98 watermelons worth a jackson* is published under De La Salle University's Malate Literary Folio Tomo XXXVII Bilang 3 (2022)

11. *contemporary corporate conditioning* 101 is published under De La Salle University's Tomo XXXVII Special Folio: Larawan ng Kasalukuyan (2021)

12. *the best medicine* is previously published under De La Salle University's Malate Literary Folio Tomo XXXVI Bilang 3 (2021)

13. An older version of *spring awakening* is published under 20 To Life Magazine Vol. 3 (2024)

14. *15 line sonnet for every floor before we reached the stars* is published in online literary magazine Mobile Data Mag (2024) *palindrome of flights (digital collage)* is published in *La Monarca* zine by Plutos (2025)

15. *parallelisms of work & love (or lack thereof)* is published in online literary short form magazine Systemic Dreaming (2025)

16. *new year, same me* is is published in online literary magazine Mobile Data Mag (2025)

# acknowledgements

This book is a mere glimpse of everything and everyone who has inspired me in my 27 years of living, for that I am eternally grateful to everyone who has been a part of my life.

Sa mga kaibigan ko sa Pilipinas, mahal ko kayong lahat. Pag-ipunan niyo pamasahe ko pauwi, thank you! To Gene & Daniel, my constants and adopted siblings. To Rolande & Caitlin/Jenelle for the most unhigned friendships. Nicky, Gian, Gana, Raisa, Panjie, Kyla, Vail, Ingrid, Gyan, Mikee, Debbie, Mike, FlowerBan Fam; MC & DLSU teammates, my fellow athlete-students, thank you for your support across the world. Kung 'di ko kayo nabanggit dito singilin niyo ako.

Maraming, maraming salamat sa lahat ng mga naging ka-staffer, editor at kaibigan ko sa Malate Literary Folio, dahil sa inyo, mas nakilala ko ang sarili ko bilang isang manlilikha at manunulat. Sa Malate ako nagsimulang magseryoso sa pagsusulat, at hanggang ngayon, baon ko pa rin ang lahat ng natutunan ko sa inyo. Muli ko kayong binabati, *gawa lang nang gawa, sining alay sa madla.*

Sa mga naging guro ko, salamat lahat ng tinuro niyo sa akin. Mananatiling buhay ang diwa ninyo sa mga tula at obrang ito. Sir Jimmy, salamat sa pangangamusta at pagsuporta, nagawa kong ipagpatuloy pagsusulat dahil sa pag-engayo niyo sa akin.

To all the amazing women who took care of me through the years: Coach Karin, my favorite neighbor carpool buddy, thank you for believing that I will grow a lot in the States. Sa lahat ng mga yaya mula nung kabataan ko, ate Jane; my softball ates, coaches and titas; Ate Kyla for always supporting and being a role model; Sarah for being my first compass in all things LA; besties of ate Sam, my second set of sisters: Helene, Nikki, Crisel thank you for showing me what women can do.

To everyone I met here so far, you all welcomed me to different parts of this city and gave it your own color in my mind. This has been the most surreal experience yet.

Maestro, for believing in my work since day one, and recommending me to be the host of La Palabra. Ingrid, for her words and wisdom that inspire me to grow. Andy for encouraging me to join CLI. Hanna, for the first open mic I ever read at. Brian, for LA Literature and his consistent championing of my poetry. To Moy for telling me that my poems are good, and that I should read slower. Thank you for always inspiring me. To Marc, Karo, Chloe, Jennifer/Miss B, Ale, Christian, Sunday Jump, Avenue 50 Studio, PSNY classmates, Ayling, and everyone else who believed in my work. Thank you Jesse, for taking my poetry to new places, and leading me to more lovely people I've become friends with. To Ivan, Madi, Daryl, Duncan, Rhiannon, Nikolai, Laura. I'm so grateful to have found some of the coolest poets here. Cheers!

To Lauren, you're the warmest embrace and sweetest person I've met here. Thank you for your sisterhood.

To Kuya Kirby, my number one Pamaypay, thank you so much for being a true friend. For bridging the cultural gap I have between (Immigrant) Filipino culture and American culture, helping me understand how to relate and live with people here, and always being there throughout many crises I've gone through the past year.

To the village who has brought this book into its own Becoming. At first, I wanted to do everything on my own but when I began welcoming people to this house of poems, it changed and grew more beautifully. It became *alive.*

To the *best* cover designer who brought my vision to a whole new world with the wonders of her mind. Ja, maraming salamat sa pagbigay mo ng kulay at buhay sa librong ito.

To my CLI Class and mentors: Kialya, TK, Bonifer, Leila, Carlos, Betty, Frank, Quinoaa (and Toku!), Dianne, Tasha, Darryl, Monica, Adrianne, La Neta, Emily, AKoldPiece and Hiram. To my proofreader, Teresa, and interior designer Kallie. Being the youngest in the class, I've learned so much about growing up staying true to myself. I cannot thank you all for that.

To the Riot of Roses family: the embodiment of the saying *"behind every successful woman, are more successful women lifting each other up."* To Anastasia and Analicia for choosing to publish my book, helping me with all the edits I need, pushing me to bring this book to life in its most beautiful form. To Brenda, for being an inspiration. Right when I read your book I thought, *I want her to publish my book.* Your words came right when I needed it. Thank you so much for your patience and guidance throughout this whole process.

To Nikki, my forever roomie, teammate, sister, best friend. You are a blessing, a sunflower that always brightens up my world, no matter how far apart we are. There is no poem I can ever write that can fully embody how much you mean to me. We've seen each other grow for so many years, and I'm beyond grateful to always have you with me through it all. You're my lucky star. Thank you for being my pillar. I love you so much, alam mo na yan!

To Jasey, my bestie and sister for as long as I can remember. We've seen each other through so many haircuts (I've even cut your hair too), music phases, and now new work phases. I can't wait to see you again and grow older with you. I love you and all your worms!

To my family: my mom for being the strongest woman I wish to be; my dad for teaching me to love all forms of art, music, and taking pictures of me when I did not see beauty in myself; to my siblings, ate Sam for being my guidepost- from childhood to college, I followed your footsteps until I've found my own way. Kuya Jam for the food, pastries, astrophotography, folk music, and keeping me grounded by annoying me every day since I moved here, and Tam, my fellow artist sibling, for sharing your clothes, the latest K-pop, constructive creative advice, and annoying me remotely as well. To Ringo, Jagger, and Maddie, thank you for being my reason to keep working, I love you all.

To the kids looking for themselves in their mirrors,
this book is yours, as much as it is mine.

## about the artist

Unbecoming, Swimming Ladies, Gorjaz Gorlz, page inserts, and back cover are created by Justine Gabriela "Ja" S. Amores.

Ja is a visual artist based in Baguio, Philippines. She derives her inspirations from the extensive research and readings, experiences from her travels, conversations with young and old people. Her themes mostly dwells on gorl kween energy, Filipino indigenous culture and dreams in diaspora. She has illustrated for a children's book on Cordillera weaving and participated in group exhibitions. She recently participated in Manila Illustration Fair and Jakarta Illustration & Creative Arts Fair.

Ja's painting companions are her two lovely cats, Floki and Amigo.
Instagram: @esoiuqetsel
Website: https://readymag.website/u413952925/4375182/

## about the author

Pam Concepcion is an interdisciplinary artist from Quezon City, Philippines. She delves into whatever creative medium she can learn, like poetry, screenwriting, graphic design, collages, video editing, and more. Her writing is influenced by the many books, poetry, music, song lyrics, movies, TV shows, screenplays, and visual art she has absorbed, her thirteen years playing softball, her educational background, and exposure to the local arts and music scene around Metro Manila. She loves exploring how complex sociopolitical or socioeconomic phenomena intimately affect our relationships with ourselves, friends, loves, family, and everyone else around us.

Pam began writing poetry for friends in her high school days. She studied Industrial Engineering and minored in Communications and New Media at De La Salle University-Manila. Later, she joined the university's *Malate Literary Folio* organization where she first published her poetry. In 2023, she moved to Los Angeles County, began reading at open mics, and joined Community Literature Initiative (USC Chapter 11) where she put this book together. *Unbecoming*, her first published book, is a culmination of poems written throughout December 2020 to July 2025.

## about the publisher

Riot of Roses Publishing House is a radical feminist, award-winning press that was founded in 2021 to amplify the stories of historically silenced voices and narratives.

Xicana owned. Mujerista focused. For the people.

We publish books that heal and liberate.

Read our rebellion.

Find & follow us @riotofrosespublishing
Visit us at www.riotofrosespublishinghouse.com

www.ingramcontent.com/pod-product-compliance
Ingram Content Group UK Ltd.
Pitfield, Milton Keynes, MK11 3LW, UK
UKHW062312290726
14090UKWH00018B/1033